X. 199.
36

TED DEXTER'S LITTLE CRICKET BOOK

TED DEXTER'S LITTLE CRICKET BOOK

Ted Dexter
with Ralph Dellor

BLOOMSBURY

First published in Great Britain 1996
Bloomsbury Publishing Plc, 2 Soho Square, London W1V 6HB

Copyright © 1996 by Ted Dexter

The moral right of the author has been asserted

Illustrations by Rob Perry

A CIP catalogue record for this book is available
from the British Library

ISBN 0 7475 2534 X

10 9 8 7 6 5 4 3 2 1

Typeset by Hewer Text Composition Services, Edinburgh
Printed by Clays Limited, St Ives plc

CONTENTS

~

The Incomparable Off-Spinner

The game of cricket has changed over the years, even if it has not changed as much as some people would have you believe. There might be slower over rates, there are invariably three or four fast bowlers in a side, and there is more short-pitched bowling in the modern game as opposed to previous times. However, it is my belief that the essentials do not change. The mechanics of hitting the ball or propelling the ball have not changed. The eternal truths of cricket remain unaltered.

I like to think that I am not one of those crusty old players who looks at the modern game with an air of desperation and exasperation. Cricket is a game to be enjoyed, whoever is playing in whatever era. Having said that, there are times when I wonder why young players do not want to copy the old masters when they could learn so much and become better cricketers.

The modern off-spinner is a case in point. I was fortunate to play in two Test Matches at the start of my career with the incomparable J. C. Laker. I can pay no greater compliment to Jim beyond saying that when you saw him bowl, you wondered why any off-spinner would contemplate bowling in a different fashion. He made it all look so simple. An easy, controlled approach to the wicket; a little skip into the delivery, during which the head was held high; pivot round the front foot as his arm came over; and – as important as anything which went before – he completed his action. There was nothing fancy but it was so effective.

As the new boy in the team, when I played with him in Australia in 1958–59, I was occasionally posted at short-leg. I felt very privileged to be there, although I must admit the move might well have been born of desperation. I certainly remember fielding in the deep at Sydney when the batsman swept a ball from Jim towards deep square-leg. The young Dexter failed to get any sight of the ball. I stood there gazing into space, as can happen with a large crowd as the backdrop. Eventually I started to move in one direction, only to find the ball was some thirty yards the other way. We have all seen it happen, and the fielder looks pretty silly. Jim was a past master at looking extremely disgruntled and so making you look even more foolish. Nothing too demonstrative – that was not his style – but from a distance of seventy yards he could express a withering sentiment by just a hitch of the trousers, a deep sigh and a throw of the head.

The move to short-leg was not an obvious success in that I did not actually hold a catch off his bowling. I did, however, get the opportunity to watch the batsmen trying to deal with him from the very best vantage point. There is an interesting comparison between the first ball a batsman receives in modern cricket to the first ball a batsman would get from Jim Laker. The modern off-spinner tends to bowl the first ball to a new batsman faster and flatter than usual. The ball

JIM LAKER: When you saw him bowl, you wondered why any off-spinner would contemplate bowling in a different fashion.

invariably darts in towards leg-stump. Jim's welcome to the newcomer was the opposite. He flighted the ball at the best of times, but I clearly remember standing at short-leg watching the batsman's eyes lift up and his feet shuffle uncertainly as he attempted to deal with a teasing, looped first delivery.

I know which type of ball I would prefer at that stage of my innings. The leg-stump dart is unlikely to turn much and has a straight trajectory. Judging the loop and then the turn is an altogether more testing proposition before the batsman has adjusted to conditions. In this way, Jim Laker did not just tease batsmen, he tortured them. Furthermore, he left me with not only a visual image of his greatness. I still have an aural image.

As I crouched down I could hear the ball coming. Now that would not be unusual for a fast bowler who gallops up to the wicket, bangs his front foot down and gives a grunt of effort as he releases the ball. For an off-spinner it was unique. Not that Jim made the noise; it was the ball spinning through the air which made a distinct whirring sound. I spoke to him about this and he explained that as he bowled he performed something of a conjuring trick. He held the ball in only the upper part of his fingers and never down at their base. Like most worthwhile cricketing skills, it took a time to master, but once he had learned to control the ball, the rate of spin increased considerably. Now he had a much more powerful weapon at his command.

It was interesting to watch the off-spinners of that era going through a daily ritual before they could bowl. The area on the inside of the top joint would be red raw after they had bowled a long spell the previous day. Before bowling again, they would treat the cracked and sore area with Friar's Balsam to stick it together to last the day. Then, in the evening, they cleaned it all off and softened it, with what I believe was castor oil, to allow it to cool and settle down overnight, before starting the treatment all over again the next day.

JIM LAKER: He performed something of a conjuring trick. He held the ball in only the upper part of his fingers and never down at the base.

I am not aware that this happens nowadays. I have asked a number of the modern generation of spinners if they have trouble with their spinning fingers. The usual reply is that they are really very lucky in that respect because they do not suffer from 'spinner's finger'. Even after bowling fifty overs in the match, they do not have the problem. I doubt, though, whether it is really a question of luck. The truth is that they grip the ball too low in their fingers and so do not really spin it. One of the few modern spinners who really does turn it, however, is the Australian Tim May. I noticed that he has a nasty looking crater at the top of his spinning finger. Is that just a coincidence? I think not.

Tim May might not be mentioned in the same breath as Jim Laker or West Indian Lance Gibbs, but he is the nearest thing we have to a bowler who thinks the same way as they did. Most off-spinners today bowl to a six-three leg-side field. With the ball not turning much and being bowled flat in towards leg-stump, it is reckoned there is only one side of the wicket on which the bowler will concede runs. The other approach is to turn it and bowl an off-stump line. Rather than worrying about being hit, this type of bowler sees that he can take wickets on both sides of the pitch. I am not offering prizes for guessing which approach appeals more to me, and which would have appealed more to Jim Laker.

It is a little eerie nowadays when we are shown film clips of cricket in the 1970s when Jim was a leading commentator for BBC Television. His commentary style was no more effusive than his bowling, with an endearing quality of dropping every 'g' from the ends of words. Hence a batsman would play 'a scintillatin innins'. But if the grammar and pronunciation might not always have been perfect, Jim's judgement of players and the game were excellent in any cricketing situation. There is something about spin bowlers which gives them this admirable ability, and I would say the same of the former leg-spinner Richie Benaud. While the game might be dominated by batsmen, TV and radio are dominated by bowlers. I once did a survey and found that bowlers held sway by a ratio of about two-and-a-half to one in commentary and press box. Perhaps the batsmen go on to lofty administration?

Do All Spinners Throw?

The first time I encountered Tony Lock was as a University freshman at Cambridge in 1956. Stories were already rife about his action. I was told to watch out for his quicker ball. In the first innings of this, my baptism as a first-class cricketer, I was bowled by the quickie, Peter Loader, for nought. In the second innings, however, I managed to stay long enough to score 44 before falling to a catch by Ken Barrington off the off-spin bowling of Eric Bedser. During this knock, I faced Tony Lock and was ever vigilant for his infamous quicker ball.

Now and again he would bowl a delivery which appeared to be that bit quicker, but it was nothing that I had not come across in other forms of cricket. In those days we could talk freely to the umpires, who tended to look after us young University players. They helped us whenever possible, giving us encouragement if we did something right, or shook their heads if we strayed from the accepted way of playing. When I got to the non-striker's end, I remember asking that great character Frank Lee, the old Somerset opening bat, if I had just been on the end of Lock's quicker ball. 'Quicker ball? You'll spot the quicker ball when you get one from Lockie, don't worry about that!' Apparently Doug Insole was once comprehensively beaten by the quicker one and, as he surveyed the shattered wicket, inquired of the umpire whether it should go down as bowled Lock or run out.

It was a flat pitch at Fenner's, ideal to enable us students to stay in for an hour or so against great bowlers and thus learn a bit about what they could do. Tony Lock showed me that he could turn the ball appreciably, as match figures of 8 for 66 testified. I had heard about pitches at The Oval which were meant to be prepared specifically for Laker and Lock, and thought how it might have been facing them there as opposed to friendly Fenner's. I had also heard about the way Stuart Surridge captained Tony Lock in particular. If it was a turning pitch and he was not taking wickets, he would really let him know, geeing him up as he might have done a fast bowler. Suddenly the spin increased, there was more bounce and he would become a really formidable opponent.

Even so, it is still difficult to believe it possible that Lock could bowl at the other end twice while Jim Laker was taking his nineteen-wicket haul in the Old Trafford Test and at The Oval when he took ten wickets in an innings against the same 1956 Australians. Lock finished up with one wicket out of thirty! Asked how he felt about taking that one wicket which had denied Laker twenty in the Old Trafford Test, he replied that he was a bit annoyed about Laker taking nineteen to deprive him of all twenty.

Stories already abounded about him bending his arm to a greater or lesser extent to give him his spin and to allow every opportunity for the much quicker ball. The problem about bending the arm is that the variation of speed is much more easily disguised because there is not the same evident effort with the body. The effect is merely achieved from the elbow. However, this was all in the background at this time and nothing much was mentioned about it until the New Zealand leg of Peter May's 1958–59 tour to Australasia.

During one match, we were invited to visit the New Zealand captain's house where, after dinner, John Reid put on a little film show. He had brought back some good quality cine film from their previous summer's tour of England. The lights were dimmed and suddenly there was the old 8mm film of the match at Lord's, taken from the players' balcony. We saw Tony Lock running in to bowl, but in very slow motion. Perhaps the cameras had just become a little more sophisticated because it was sharp and clear, and from the very first ball there was a pronounced bending and straightening of the arm, along with an absolute roar of mirth from all concerned.

There was much hilarity from the England players but, when the lights went up again, there was an absolutely ashen-faced Tony Lock. If not actually speechless, he was not prepared to speak to anybody as he was obviously deeply shocked and affected by what he had seen. It is likely that he had not seen his action before in such slow motion, or perhaps from that particular angle. He retired from the gathering.

Next day he came down to the ground, went into the nets and simply bowled donkey drops as he desperately attempted to keep his arm straight. Only then would he start to speak about what he had seen. He claimed he had no idea about the way in which he was bowling and certainly was not prepared to continue in similar fashion. It needed a good deal of cajoling merely to get him to bowl anything like presentably for the rest of the game.

He went back to Surrey to work on his action, reverting to a slower, more orthodox delivery. It took him some time to come to terms with it, but eventually he succeeded and got back into the England team. He came to India and Pakistan on my tour in 1961–62 and was a wonderful competitor. Into his thirties, knees strapped up, he gave his all. He would willingly bowl all day, but more than that, in those hot, dry conditions he left me with two abiding memories. He would always come off the field absolutely covered in dust from head to foot because he had hurled himself around after the ball all day, and as a result would regularly win the fielding prize without opposition. In those days when they used to decorate the chosen player with a garland made of rupees, Tony Lock invariably had his garland at the end of the day.

He was not selected for my 1962–63 tour to Australia, but instead went to play for Western Australia in the Sheffield Shield. Back to Surrey, and England, in 1963, he then settled in Perth before returning to county cricket with Leicestershire between 1965 and 1967. He was a great success as captain of both Western Australia and his adopted county, and even answered an emergency by flying to the Caribbean to play his final two Tests in 1967–68.

Playing for Western Australia, he took wickets against

us on that 1962–63 tour in Perth. It was one of the fastest and bounciest pitches in the world, yet here was what was by now an orthodox left-arm spinner being particularly successful. There was not another spinner in Australia nearly as effective as he was. However, a question remains. Did he completely modify his action or did he just bowl slower and retain his powers of spin?

He had been successful on England's uncovered pitches, but until then had met with little success overseas, as I remember from the 1958–59 tour of Australia. The less the ball turned, the more he tried to spin it. What actually happened was that he tried to bowl it faster, and that resulted in even less turn. The Australians treated him as a straight bowler and, with his angle of approach, would just whip him through mid-wicket. Then he tried to pitch it a bit wider and was hit on both sides of the wicket.

The story goes that originally he had been an orthodox slow left-armer but that, one winter, he went into indoor nets at Croydon which had a low ceiling. He could not toss it up as he had always done, rather being forced to lower his arm and fire it through. He found that he could spin it quite a lot more, without knowing how. That leads us on to the question of whether all spinners who really turn the ball adopt the same technique as the 'Mark II' Tony Lock, with the same innocence?

I do not suppose there have been many of the real spinners who bowl with an absolutely rigid arm as does the fast bowler. I doubt whether there have been more than one in ten slow bowlers who have not bent the arm at all. Of course, this does not mean that they all throw, because the crucial factor is whether they straighten the arm again. If they maintain the bend in the arm throughout the action, it is quite legitimate; it is only if the arm straightens that they break the Law. If it is bent, there is the tendency to straighten it a little bit and the opportunity to straighten it a lot from time to time. One type will not be very obvious from the other. I suggest that all the big spinners of the ball use that rotation of the shoulder and elbow to a greater or lesser extent.

Another question arises, as to whether any of the big spinners have ever bowled with a consistently straight arm? Lance Gibbs, perhaps, but I have never seen Lance Gibbs in slow motion. He had a very whirly type of action, and I can visualise him bending the elbow a little after he had let the ball go, which is perfectly acceptable.

Even those bowlers who bowl with their arm slightly bent throughout are not infringing the Law, but I believe that in some way they have a better rotation from the shoulder. Furthermore, whenever slow bowlers are talking about their actions, they tend to demonstrate with a bent arm. When casually describing a type of delivery, they make no attempt to do so with anything other than a throwing action.

Fred Titmus was another off-spin bowler who, I reckon, would have been eligible to join the straight-arm brigade. Even if he was not a big turner of the ball, he did have a nice flight and could do just enough to keep the batsman guessing. From the same era, Ray Illingworth could well have had a little bit of elbow action, but Jim Laker was certainly straight, and John Emburey could also be counted amongst the straight-arm spinners. This indicates that there have been some slow bowlers who have reached the top without bending the bowling arm, but there are plenty who, it must be said, bend the arm just a little bit more during the action.

The Indian off-spinner Erapally Prasanna went through a wonderfully successful period for a while. He had a delightful flight and great powers of spin, but he also looked a little suspect from time to time. Two Sri Lankans, Muralitharan and Warnaweera, reach the extremes of credibility in my opinion, as does the Indian Rajesh Chauhan, with at least those of his deliveries which spin most. That difference in action leaves the umpires in a very difficult position. It has never been particularly obvious to the naked eye, to the extent that the umpire can see the arm go from bent to straight. It is something the umpire might sense but, if he just senses it, he has to ask himself whether that was a throw. By the time he has made up his mind, the moment has perhaps passed.

I remember in my second season at Cambridge we played the West Indians, including Sonny Ramadhin. He bowled leg-breaks and off-breaks with a strange action that included finger-spin, but the ball appeared to come from the back of the hand. Our captain, Gammy Goonesena, was a fine leg-break bowler himself and told us to play Ram entirely as an off-break bowler; if he turned one the other way, it would probably be quite gently and we would just have to hope we missed it. By the number of times he hit Peter May and Colin Cowdrey on the pads while they put on 411 for the fourth wicket at Edgbaston in 1957, it appears that it was the right strategy to play Ramadhin as an off-spinner.

As great a bowler as he was, it has to be said that his arm probably bent during the delivery. Ramadhin always bowled with his sleeves buttoned down, and that makes it easier to disguise a bend. I hasten to add that Ramadhin and all the others were not aware of breaking the Laws of Cricket as they bowled, even if they did. I would say the same about the faster bowlers who have 'thrown'. The difference, however, is that the quicks are striving for more pace and bounce while the spinners seek more turn. Emotionally, there is not such a problem with spinners, but when a batsman gets hit without being able to pick up the delivery because of the change of pace, emotions run high. Being cynical, perhaps, we batsmen always used to say that we did not really mind a bowler throwing as long as he did it slowly.

'Run-Stealers Flickering To and Fro'

What is the connection between running between wickets and heavy bats? The best run-stealers in my time were those who could really control the pace of the ball off the bat by simply dropping it into the right area just a few yards away and going through for a single that appeared almost leisurely. That was all part of their all-round cricketing skill, but the advent of heavy bats has made this something of a lost art. So who were the very good ones that come to mind?

Bobby Simpson and Bill Lawry, who opened together so often for Australia during the 1960s, were among the very best. They might not have been greyhounds as individuals but, as a pair, they were wonderful at rotating the strike and keeping the score moving with well-judged runs. Lawry was better at dropping the ball on the left-hander's off side where you had the right-arm over-the-wicket bowler following through on the other side of the pitch. He was not a cutter, so the short ball outside the off-stump would be just dropped down and another single went on to the total without any risk being taken. The right-handed Simpson favoured dropping the ball on the leg side, once again away from the bowler following through. These are skills which do not seem to be quite as well rehearsed among the current generation.

If I were asked to name the worst runners between wickets, there are one or two names from recent England

ROBIN SMITH: I wondered whether the big, early pick-up of the heavy bat makes it virtually impossible just to drop the ball where required?

Test teams who would feature. Graham Gooch and Robin Smith, for all their other admirable qualities, have not impressed me with their running. I remember watching recordings of those two batting and, on two hours of tape, there was not a quick single in the entire partnership. I wondered whether the big, early pick-up of the heavy bat makes it virtually impossible just to drop the ball where required, especially on the forward strokes?

Some of the good runners between wickets have been good simply because they were fast over the ground. When you get two of those in together, the fielders' job becomes virtually impossible. Another Australian, Dean Jones, when he really got going and found a willing partner, could destroy a fielding side simply by turning the ones into twos and twos into threes, to say nothing of finding singles that others might not contemplate. This frustrated the bowlers, they got angry and could not bowl properly.

Then, of course, there are those batsmen with whom it is a delight to run. In my England time Colin Cowdrey was the best man with whom to run. That might surprise some people, because he was certainly no greyhound, but his sense of a run was impeccable and you always knew there was a safe single when he called it. There was not any need to check if the ball had gone far enough. That is the trick of running well between wickets. You have to trust one another; when one calls the other is already on his way.

On the other side of the coin are those players with whom you would rather not be running. I never saw the worst of Denis Compton in that respect, but anyone who could run out his brother for nought in his benefit match has to be high on the list of the least desirable partners. The old stories are always the best, but it was said that the first two calls from Denis were just a matter of opening negotiations. The third one was probably 'goodbye'.

Geoffrey Boycott was a terrible partner to run with because he always had to double-check. You called him for a run and he was looking at the ball, not at you, and not taking the call on trust. He had many victims and I think I might be able to claim to be the first. It was at Port Elizabeth in the Fifth Test of the 1964–65 tour, when the young Geoffrey was so intense that he could only think of staying there, not of scoring. Then at the end of every other over he would think that he ought to get a single. That resulted in a push off the last ball and a run. I was always taught to go if called but, after a while, the fielders had closed in. He still called me, I went haring through only to find that he had hardly set off, and he managed to get his foot back in the crease before I had passed by. I saw a little look from him which said, 'I don't think I'm out.' He did go on to make 117 after I had been run out for 40, only the third time I suffered such a fate in 102 Test innings. I felt that some of my efforts to befriend him on that trip were not repaid in the best possible way.

Nor has Mike Gatting always been totally reliable as a runner. I do not know what it is, but he sometimes seems to lack concentration in that aspect of the game. He will turn the wrong way, fail to look properly, and the result has been some nasty mix-ups at crucial moments which affected the outcome of a match. Gatting would stand in contrast to some of the greyhounds thrown up by one-day cricket. Neil Fairbrother would be high on the list with the best. Push and run, push and run, hit and run; it is amazing, when you start doing it, just what you can get away with. If both batsmen genuinely go, there is almost nothing the fielders can do to stop them.

Having said that, there is a point when the run, rather than the stopping of it, becomes impossible. I remember feeling that the Sussex running between wickets had been weak. As captain, I ordered a really stiff running between wickets session to see what could be achieved. We set the fielders back and then brought them in progressively. By the end of the session we were getting more run-outs than completed runs. It did not prove anything very much, except that you cannot just do it by numbers. It is a matter of trust and understanding.

One of the Sussex players who was particularly good was Mike Griffith. He was not only fast over the ground, but he was extremely agile and could stop and turn with remarkable speed. Time is usually lost at the ends when, having run twenty yards, you have to stop and come back again. Just as a swimmer tries to perfect the turn, so does the good runner. Griffith was particularly good at that, wasting little time. He was also a brilliant hockey player, and so was used to running, stopping and turning. He also gained a rackets Blue at Cambridge.

Obviously there is the business of putting pressure on the outfielder. If you start to come back for the second run, he only needs to make a little fumble to let you get home. Conversely, the fielder who is having a bad time can egg the batsmen on. I remember in 1964–65 in South Africa how Colin Bland was not only a fantastic fielder but also extremely fast between the wickets. I was not as quick at thirty as I had been at twenty and he was taking twos to me down at third-man whenever he could during the Third Test at Newlands. I rather resented this. I let him have a couple of runs by moving quickly but not really giving it everything. 'This time,' I thought. As he hit it I was on the move and, despite the fact he realised he was in trouble, he thought he would take me on but a nice, flat, one-bounce throw put an end to that.

As schoolboys, we were taught that there were only three calls: 'yes', 'no', and 'wait'. Moving up into University cricket and then county cricket, I encountered a whole new variety of calls. Many were simply affectations: 'Come one'; 'run'; 'come two' all came into common currency despite the fact that they often lead to confusion. Then, in Test cricket, you have to run with people with whom you have never batted before. If they have different conventions in their county and start to take a run without saying anything, all sorts of problems can result. I had one nightmare experience with Gilbert Parkhouse of Glamorgan in one of my early Tests, against India at Old Trafford in 1959. He kept setting off for runs without any warning, but it did not stop him suggesting that the lack of communication was my fault. I had been brought up on what I still believe is the best system: the three calls.

'Yes', 'no', and 'wait' served me pretty well throughout my career, but there was one bad running incident which I remember with shame. It happened in Kanpur on the 1961–62 tour of India. Kenny Barrington was well on his way to the first double-century of his Test career.

We were following-on, but there was nothing in the pitch, there was plenty of time, and he was in his element, accumulating his runs. He had scored 172 without undue alarm and I was also comfortable with a hundred to my name. I really just wanted to keep the strike because, when I hit one out into the covers, I did not immediately set off for the single, yet it was such a long one that I eventually thought I had to. Even then, my heart was not really in it. The fielders moved on to it, Kenny was halfway down, but I sent him back and left him stranded.

That apart, I felt I was generally a reasonable runner, being quite quick over the ground. Undoubtedly my finest hour in this respect was on the last day of the Melbourne Test of 1962–63 when we scored 237 for three wickets to beat Australia. I put on 124 for the second wicket with Rev. David Sheppard. For once it was two England batsmen who ran the Australian fielders ragged. From Sussex partnerships, I knew David was an excellent judge of a run, just working the ball into the spaces. The pitch by that stage was not the type for expansive strokes, and it was our running which got us into a winning position. We rattled the bowlers, rattled the fielders, and rattled up the runs. Ironically enough, only two wickets were lost on that final day. I was run out for 52 and The Reverend was also run out, for 113, when the scores were level.

Running between the wickets was one of Don Bradman's major accomplishments. He was not just an extremely aggressive batsman but he was one of the early ones to set store by running between the wickets to get full value from his strokes and those of his partners. It helped him to keep the strike, and all the great batsmen want to stay at the business end. You do not score many from the non-striker's end but, with proper attention to an often neglected art, many runs can be gained in perfect safety from right under the fielder's nose.

Mr Personality

Fred Trueman is a character. Stories abound about him being the aggressive, cantankerous Yorkshireman, and many of these stories emanate from the man himself. In truth he is really Mr Personality, and never more so than on the field. Without being extravagant in the things he did, he was a wonderful showman. With the mere toss of his splendid black hair, he could transmit exactly what he thought of a batsman. He could communicate with the crowd, getting them on his side, and even against him if he wanted to gee them up.

Aggression was not necessary for him on the field because the quality of his bowling did the talking for him when he was in his pomp. The word 'pomp' is always used in association with Fred. Defined in the dictionary as 'splendid display', it does very well to sum up the man at the height of his considerable powers. It was the time he spent in the opposition dressing-room, especially in county matches when he spent more time in there than in his own, that marked him out as a pugnacious character. 'Well, what have we here? I'll have you, you and you . . .' and, glancing round the room a little further . . . 'and you two as well. I should be in for a "five for" today.' Then he would look around again, as if to make sure he had not missed anyone before pretending to spot the most timorous batsman trying to appear invisible in the corner. 'Hang on a minute . . . Make that "six for"!'

He had a wonderful Test career, based on solid foundations. He was superbly athletic and immensely

FRED TRUEMAN: With the mere toss of his splendid black hair, he could transmit exactly what he thought of a batsman.

strong, without ever being skinny fit. He always kept a bit of flesh on him, but had the strength to carry it. He has maintained those qualities to this day for, despite a considerably belly on him, I reckon he could still run up and fire a few balls down while looking like a bowler. That cannot be said for many of his age.

Furthermore, he had a glorious sideways action. There was a time when I really thought there never had been a real sideways action and it had all been a part of my imagination. An entire generation has dispensed with the concept. Then, one inspirational moment not so long ago, some old black-and-white film of Fred was shown on TV. Even if it did not appear to be quite up to the modern pace, it was wonderful to see the left arm thrown up to the sky, the shock of unruly black hair looking over the left shoulder and then the left arm sweeping down and round and up to complete a marvellous cartwheel. He even had a comment about that: 'Isn't it strange how bowlers look so much slower in black and white?'

It was this model action which got him his wickets. The full, powerful body swing and the true rotating action with a high arm gave him a natural away-swing, while the seam was upright allowing the odd one to nip back. He would get wickets caught at slip, then they started following the swing a little bit and the gate would be open for the ball to hurry through into either pad or stumps. This was never more so than in the West Indies in 1959–60 when, on wonderfully true pitches against a fine batting side, Fred took 21 wickets at 26.14. What was particularly impressive was the number of times he hit the stumps in that series – twelve times, with another five batsmen falling LBW.

There was another facet to Fred's character. He reckoned that he bowled an amazing array of deliveries to take all his wickets. He gave him this one, then that one, then his in-ducker or his yorker or whatever. Personally, I never believed much of that. All this bluster was just part of his engaging personality. I always thought that it was his basic delivery allied to his strength and the movement of the ball that got his wickets. He did not need many of the things that he occasionally imagined he did, because the straightforward, genuine article was usually good enough.

He was a very good reader of batsmen. When he was running up he would look at the batsman's feet so that he knew what they were up to and get an idea where to pitch it. I first saw him at Cambridge in one of my very early matches. I had the honour of receiving the first really sharp bouncer I had encountered from the great FST. It quite surprised me, although I can remember that I was not particularly bothered by it. As it went whizzing past I can remember thinking that it was quite lively. He banged me in the chest with another and I realised that this bowler was a bit special.

Later on I got to know him pretty well because I frequently roomed with him in Australia in 1958–59. I think they thought it would toughen up the young amateur from Cambridge if he was put in with the hard Yorkshire professional. I have always maintained that it was good fun sharing a room with Fred . . . when I could get in there. There was a period when one tended to come back and find the door locked and the fevered command from within to 'Come back a bit later, sonny.' I cannot imagine what he was up to!

Then there was Fred Trueman, the great storyteller. People used to think that he was a drinker, staying up late into the night always with a pint in his hand. That was not so. Fred was not a drinker, but he did love company. He did not want to go to bed, he wanted to chat, and one of the ways to hold his audience was with his storytelling. It must be said that he maintained a very high standard. Despite the fact that we had all heard most of the tales a hundred times over, they still seemed funny and were always beautifully told. He always managed identical inflection and timing and later on he actually worked the clubs with a similar act.

Apart from Fred the bowler, there was also Fred the close catcher. He always caught well because he always moved well to the ball. It was the position close in on the leg side to the slower bowlers that he made his own, being more at home at leg-slip than on the off side. He will be annoyed that I have not talked about his batting as well. He was not the worst, but not the best either. He tended to have a rather short backlift and a slightly agricultural bang at the ball, but when he wanted to hit it, it could go a long way. Whatever he was doing on the field, he was a never-to-be-forgotten character with whom it is a privilege to have played.

Practice Can Make Perfect

There is only one player in twenty, at all levels of the game, who is a good practiser. It is so easy to go into a net, whack away for quarter of an hour, and feel that that is the batting taken care of! When bowling, it is just a case of turning the arm over while running through the crease to make it appear quicker than it really is. To hell with what the batsman might want, you are getting the exercise for which you went. That scenario might strike a chord with club players, because it happens all over the country throughout the summer.

I have seen one or two good practice sessions. Geoffrey Boycott never let an opportunity pass by to practise properly. He used to bat with the same intensity in the nets as he did in the middle. He did not try out any fancy shots but concentrated on what he was going to do in a match. In recent times, Alec Stewart impressed me when he got the chance to open the England innings in New Zealand in 1992. He had a very structured practice. He set out to achieve something and got the bowlers to co-operate with him. He asked for one type of delivery, then another, and really used his twenty minutes to good advantage.

Bowlers tend to be somewhat sloppy when it comes to practice. I seldom see them working with someone to keep the action in good shape and to guard against laziness creeping in. They need someone watching to

GEOFFREY BOYCOTT: *He never let an opportunity pass by to*
practise properly.

ensure that they complete their action, while there is
little point in continually overstepping the crease in nets.
At worst, practising bad habits in the nets will probably
mean that they become ingrained and are taken out to
the middle. At best, you are achieving absolutely nothing
to improve your game.

Overall, the one element which cricket practices lack, and which would improve the quality of practice, is to think of ballet dancers. From the lowest member of the troupe to the prima ballerina, they all do the same practice exercises, they all go to the bar and go through the same basic routine. Only then do the very good ones give the performance their own personality. If more cricketers had such a basic routine, their practice would be more meaningful. Batsmen should check their grip, stance and pick-up, and make sure their body is in the right position. Bowlers should pay attention to their actions and use the red and white halved ball to ensure that the seam is in the right place as they bowl. If these are daily routines, when they go out into the middle it becomes an entirely different, easier game.

One of the great problems with cricket practice is that you have to make time for it. There is not time waiting to be used, like with golfers. They might spend five hours out on the course, but in the summer there are another seven or eight hours to fill. If they are not bookworms or do not have similar interests, it is almost essential to practise to occupy time. At least it keeps them out of the bar! For cricketers it is not as easy to find the time, especially these days when games start early and, after the match, they are expected to socialise with opponents and sponsors. Accepting all that, Geoffrey Boycott always found the time and others could if they made the effort.

The Lovable Bulldog

~

If I analysed my career for England, I probably batted with Kenny Barrington longer than with anyone else. I was a great admirer of him both as a batsman and as a man of character. He had an extraordinary craggy face, a fine array of teeth invariably set in a huge grin, and a great beak of a nose. With all that went a very sweet and generous underlying character as a person which was not what might be expected from as tough and doughty an opponent as could be found in world cricket.

I saw just enough of him in his early days to know that here was a terrific talent well-coached in the skills of the game. He was a strokemaker and a quality batsman, apart from being a good fielder and occasionally useful leg-break bowler. What then happened to Ken Barrington has happened to many a player trying to establish himself in Test cricket. Faced with the ultimate challenge, up against the best bowlers, initial failure brings about a change in the way batsmen go about their task. In Kenny's case, he got into the England side in 1955, played in two Tests and then was out of the team until 1959. During the interim, the iron entered his soul and he decided that the only way to get back in was through sheer weight of runs. He was going to pile up the runs at every opportunity so the selectors had to pick him.

That is a very good strategy. However, he also

decided that he had been getting out too often caught on the off side. In future he was going to cover the line of the ball more, would not be doing much cover-driving, but would get across and put himself squarely behind the ball, showing the bowler the maker's name in time-honoured fashion. There are various ways of achieving this aim. In Kenny's case, he decided to do so by playing in a much more open manner, rather than being classically sideways-on, and to open his stance to look the bowler squarely in the eye.

He succeeded in his objective, because he got back into the England side and became a fixture as a major, if not the leading, English batsman of his time. His change of style also made him a relatively slow scorer because some of his more productive shots were not there for him any more. He knew well enough that if he was going to be square-on, he was not going to be going for the cover-drives which had brought him so many runs but which had also cost him his wicket previously. It also made him more vulnerable to the ball moving off the seam and that showed itself in him being so much more successful overseas, where the pitches are harder and offer the bowler less lateral movement. He became more of a back-foot player and it took him until his eighty-first Test innings to record his first century on home soil, by which time he had already scored nine abroad.

He was always a very good player of spin, one of the better of the early sweepers, as opposed to nowadays when so many are adept at the shot. He was perhaps ahead of his time in that, and perhaps he was helped by his open stance in that he was less likely to be looking

KEN BARRINGTON: *He would get across and put himself squarely behind the ball, showing the bowler the maker's name in time-honoured fashion.*

for the drive and more likely to be in position to sweep. The other effect of setting himself so square was that he became a very big target when the fast bowlers bounced it at him. It becomes almost impossible to move laterally to get out of the way of the ball. This meant that he became quite an Aunt Sally for the West Indian quicks and they really hurt him. They hurt him not only physically, because he was always brave, but mentally. It really did get through to him and I am not surprised because of the battering he took.

There are perhaps similarities between Ken Barrington and Robin Smith in that respect. Robin came into the England team as a big strong hitter of the ball who was going to cut and pull and drive and play all the shots. He immediately got into trouble with the short ball and went to hook a few times against quicker bowling with more bounce and got himself out. He did not want to lose his place and so he decided to cut out the hook. Without that as a weapon he was in even more strife to the short ball angled in. Not wanting to take his eye off the ball, the next development was the exaggerated lean-back to avoid the bouncer. It is all Robin's own system, 'doing the limbo' to get out of the way of the ball. I remember seeing him practise by getting people to throw the ball underarm, but hard, at his head from short of a length.

I could not help feeling that this was going to end in tears. It did in as much that he sustained a nasty blow from Ian Bishop at Old Trafford in the 1995 Test against the West Indies. That was an edged shot into his face, but his style does tend to make him a little late on the ball and prevents him from getting into the best position from which to play. Now we have another batsman who is nothing like the swashbuckling player of old but who, nonetheless, has become a relatively successful battler.

It is interesting to contemplate why there are so many more instances of batsmen getting hit on the head in modern cricket. Perhaps the bowlers are faster and generally bowl shorter. It might be that the introduction of helmets has resulted in a fall in levels of technique by batsmen when it comes to avoiding the bouncer. Most likely it is a combination of both, although it should be remembered that the average height of fast bowlers has increased dramatically. This means that they can make the ball bounce head high from further up the pitch, giving the batsmen less time to get out of the way. With some of the very tall ones, there is a balloon effect, while the shorter ones bowl a skidding bouncer which will stay at head height for longer. It makes life very uncomfortable for the batsman and is why a number are forced to modify their approach once they reach Test level.

Having decided to curb his natural attacking flair, there was one occasion when Ken Barrington decided to favour adventure instead of circumspection. In 1963 Wesley Hall and Charlie Griffith were at full power for the West Indies and by the time the second innings at The Oval came round we were assured of defeat in the series. Kenny suddenly came out with a bold statement to the rest of the team: 'I'm bloody well fed up with spending all my time ducking and weaving. I'm going to get after that Charlie Griffith and I'm going to hook him this time.' In 1963 The Oval was not as fast as it became in later years, and it was Kenny's home ground, but we still looked forward to the promise of a great spectacle.

Kenny had moved carefully to 20 when the contest began in earnest as Charlie Griffith came on to bowl. He dropped the first ball short and Kenny swivelled to send it like a rifle bullet through mid-wicket for four. Charlie stood there like an angry bull. He went back and raced in to deliver a much faster short ball. Kenny went for the hook again, got a top edge as it sped on to him, and scored four more first bounce to the sightscreen behind him. The angry bull was now injured and even more dangerous. The ground shook as he thundered in and let go one of his really quick specials. Kenny was in position to hook again, only to find that he was on the receiving end of a lethal, 100mph yorker. It was outside leg-stump, hit Kenny straight on the toe and cannoned off to remove the middle and leg stumps from the ground. Kenny hurled his bat away and threw away his glove as he grabbed his injured toes. He was hopping around on one foot before realising that he had to get back on to two feet, collecting his scattered equipment and trailing off in undignified and painful manner. It probably did not help to be met by the entire England team manning the dressing-room balcony convulsed in laughter. It was not long before he joined in to laugh at himself.

Despite his general bonhomie and humour, Ken Barrington was also highly strung and intense. This meant that he did not sleep too well when Test Matches were being played. In Australia in 1962–63, the manager was none other than Bernard, Duke of Norfolk – another known insomniac. During the Melbourne Test, Kenny called the manager during the middle of the night to say that he was tossing and turning and could get no sleep. The Duke, responding to his managerial duties just as he might have responded to a command in his other guise as Lord Marshal of England, immediately offered to take what were reputed to be some good sleeping pills to Ken's room. It happened that the team was staying in a huge Victorian edifice with lots of staircases, corridors, and different levels. His Grace set off in search of the relevant room, only to find that the lifts had stopped and there was nobody around to give him directions to a room some half-a-mile of passage away. After going up and down and all around, he eventually located the Barrington room. However, he had taken so long to reach him that Kenny had fallen into a deep sleep and failed to hear the knock on the door.

Kenny was a great man to have on tour when things became a little oppressive. It can be a little trying when playing in front of big crowds like in India, Pakistan or the West Indies as they become rather vociferous and can try to get at individuals. It is of tremendous value to have someone on your side who can communicate with the crowd. They have to be a little larger than life, because the subtlety of a small gesture is lost; it needs someone to be funny in a big way. Kenny could make the expansive gesture and charm the crowd.

He probably felt a bit less restricted when playing overseas than when at home. The pitches tended to suit him, and he was a good player of leg-spin because he was such a good sweeper. As an indication of his uninhibited approach overseas, he more than once went to his hundred with a six. I cannot imagine him doing that in England under the watchful gaze of the full selection committee. Remember, he was dropped from the side after taking 437 minutes to score 137 against New Zealand at Edgbaston in 1965. Nowadays we are so grateful for centuries from English batsmen that they can take forever without suffering such a reprimand.

A great enthusiast and joker, he loved to get involved in any prank going, and initiated most himself. After the 1961–62 tour of India, he brought back a number of their cricket balls which were like round, red stones, they were so hard. At Surrey pre-season practice nets, he waited until little Bernard Constable went in to bat. He took with him an old bat with which to get going, and a brand new bat to knock in when he felt in some sort of form. Kenny waited until he changed over bats before getting out his new Indian ball. He tossed up a head high full toss which Bernie Constable could not resist. He went for the big hit, made contact and looked down to see a big hole in the middle of his new bat. It had all gone exactly as planned by Kenny in India some months before.

He certainly became the bulwark of English batting and it was always said that, when he came out, he was the one batting for England with a Union Jack for a shirt. We had so much fun with him and he was such a genuinely lovable guy that it was sometimes forgotten how often he had got England out of the muck. It was very sad when we lost him at the age of fifty in 1981 because he was doing a great job with the England team as one of the early coach-managers. English cricket might be in a much healthier state in international terms if Kenny Barrington had been around longer to pass on the fine qualities of which he had so many.

Slow Bowlers Should Bowl Slowly

~

I always enjoyed the challenge of facing that great West Indian off-spinner, Lance Gibbs. He was one of the few tall spinners who could still manage to toss the ball up in teasing flight. His action had little of the classical approach for a bowler of his type. Not for him was the bound, the sideways action and the pivot around a braced front leg. He would almost bowl within his run from a chest-on position, yet his long fingers allowed him to impart serious spin on the ball, while his control and variation of pace made him a formidable opponent.

He was a great attacking bowler who never let you settle. When I went down the wicket to him or cut him, he would still want to wage war by giving the ball air and teasing me. At Lord's in 1963 I had been softened up with a sharp blow under the left knee from Charlie Griffith in the first innings. In the second innings I had limited movement – a point not lost on Gibbs. Up the ball went, I moved towards a cover drive for four, but I never got there. It turned through the gate and did me. Dexter, bowled Gibbs, 2.

Lance Gibbs had very much his own way of bowling. His 'loopy' arm and a grip which involved holding the ball in the first three fingers rather than the first two owed little to the orthodox way of bowling off-spin. But the key to his greatness was the fact that this tall man could still flight the ball.

It is an interesting point that cricketers in general have got quite a bit taller on average during my time of watching and playing the game. From my early days in the game there were several really quite short spin bowlers like Fred Titmus, 'Bomber' Wells, Sam Cook, and Doug Slade, while 'Tich' Freeman, of course, had become something of a legend. I would have thought that the average height of cricketers over the last forty-odd years might well have gone up by four or five inches. Then there is the extra length of arm to consider, which could account for another two or three inches, so in some cases the ball is being delivered from nearly a foot higher.

We have all come across schoolboy cricketers who have the most delightful loop in their delivery. They have good control over the flight and can drop the ball on a length. They often get into the 1st XI at an early age but then, over the course of a few months during the winter, they shoot up. Suddenly, the same trajectory turns into a full toss. They try to drag it down and the spin has gone, while attempts to flight it result in lobs rather than loop and a career of exciting promise is finished.

Critics of the modern game will often be heard voicing opinions about the lack of foot movement of the modern batsmen when facing spinners. The answer lies, I think, not with the batsmen, but with the bowlers, and is linked to this question of height. The spinners tend to be bowling the ball quicker because the looped trajectory is not generally available to the taller spinner. Perhaps bigger hands give more opportunity to spin the ball, but there is still an optimum pace for slow bowlers. That takes me into another topic entirely.

Certainly during my time in the game I never heard anyone talking about a bowler's optimum pace of delivery. It would have been far too scientific to talk in terms of so many feet per second. It has always been a matter of judgement, whereas it might not be a bad idea for bowlers to know at what sort of speed they are likely to get the best results. Things like pitch conditions naturally come into the equation, but it would be a good idea to know the starting point from which adjustments might be made.

Not having made a scientific study myself, my impression as an observer nowadays is that spinners tend to bowl too quickly. They do not really pose a problem for the batsmen. I watched Philip Tufnell bowling for Middlesex against the 1995 West Indians. I had enjoyed splendid hospitality in the glorious sunshine, making me bold enough to ring the dressing-room and have a conversation which went something like:

'Hi, Tuffers. I'm sorry you're not in the England side.'

'Yes, so am I, Chairman . . . (although ex-Chairman would have been more accurate by that stage!) . . . but I'm doing my best.'

'I reckon it must be costing you around £50,000 a year, to say nothing of your nice Porsche. But if you keep on bowling as quickly as you were before lunch, I reckon you can kiss goodbye to the car and all that money.'

I went round and had a chat to him on the subject.

It was probably a bit cheeky not to talk to his captain, Mike Gatting, before doing so, but Tuffers and I agreed between us that he would try to settle down and do everything a bit slower. I did not tell him to flight the ball or anything, but just to be a little more relaxed and take more time over everything he was doing. Would you believe it? The very first ball he bowled after lunch went another three feet higher than it had at any time before. The batsman rushed down the pitch and missed it; and so did the wicketkeeper!

Nevertheless, Philip Tufnell did persist in his slower mode and took six wickets, including Lara's, during the innings and got himself noticed by the media, at least. That performance against the tourists put him back among the contenders for the England side. He must have come into quite close reckoning for the left-arm spinner's place in the touring party which was chosen to go to South Africa at the end of the season. In the end it went to Richard Illingworth, another bowler who had profited from giving the ball more air and bowling more slowly than in his early days. He got a wicket with his first ball in Test cricket, but did not look likely to take too many more on flat pitches against top batsmen. How many more spinners could benefit from the slower style adopted by Richard Illingworth and, dramatically, by Philip Tufnell on that scorching summer's day at Lord's?

Silly, Silly Fields

One of the most important duties of the captain is to be helpful to his bowlers. If he wants to get the best out of them he needs to ensure that they are happy with the field to which they are bowling, and that it is encouraging them to bowl as well as they can. I have witnessed plenty of instances in recent years when the bowler is not getting the help he should expect from the skipper. I refer to the slow bowler who is burdened with the apparently obligatory fielders in those positions which, by their names, always cause mirth to small schoolboys. In this instance, I regard silly mid-off and silly mid-on as living up to their nomenclature in every respect.

A spinner who is dependent on getting ricochets off the pads to the men stationed close in on the off or leg sides will, inevitably, bowl too quickly. Bowled at the sort of pace that the spinner should deliver the ball, it is unlikely to bounce far enough for these silly fielders to come into play, even if the batsman does get a nick. This is all too common for my liking, and I have three grisly recollections to support my view.

When the Middlesex and England left-arm spinner Phil Edmonds began his career, I saw him bowling quite beautifully at Cambridge University. It was the best bit of slow bowling I had seen for ages and I thought at the time that I was watching a future England player. For once I was right. He displayed all the virtues of wonderful flight, good control and a bit of spin. The next time I saw him he was picked to play his first game for England at Headingley in 1975 against Australia in the match which was abandoned due to the activities of those who claimed George Davies was innocent.

Even before the vandals struck, it was a damp pitch offering plenty of turn to the spinners. In my opinion Phil Edmonds did not bowl particularly well in the first innings, but he did take five wickets for 28 from 20 overs which was a great start to a Test career. Within a matter of weeks, I saw him bowl again on an absolutely flat pitch at The Oval. Tony Greig was captain, called up his left-arm spinner, and set the field. It does not seem quite so strange now, but at the time it was a culture shock as I saw Greig himself go and stand no more than three yards from the bat on the off side from the outset. I could almost feel the tension in the young Phil Edmonds. Of course, there was no flight, and the ball was whizzed in at the leg stump. It was the start of what has been a sad episode for the spinners.

The way people play nowadays, cricket has definitely changed. There appears to be no such thing as a back stroke to a slow bowler. The batsman thrusts his front leg down the pitch and, if it is a length ball, the bat is tucked in behind the pad with no attempt to play the ball. It is simply kicked away. The authorities have had a look at the LBW Law, trying to produce a form of words to prevent this happening, but it has proved impossible. The umpires take the view that the bat is in line with the ball, so if it did not hit the pad, the ball would hit the bat and not the wicket.

While this has undoubtedly been a factor in the style of batting against the spinner, the captains and bowlers themselves have had a detrimental effect by their field placements. This was illustrated at Sydney in 1987 when I saw Phil Edmonds bowling in tandem with his Middlesex colleague John Emburey. England's opening bowlers had nipped in with a couple of wickets. Then the spinners were brought on, found some turn, and immediately silly mid-on and silly mid-off were put in position. Edmonds took Allan Border's wicket early in his spell, but then the bowlers kept on hitting the front pad, arms were thrown into the air and the batsmen stayed. I thought it was safe to go off for a game of golf. When I returned to the ground some four hours later, the same bowlers were bowling to Dean Jones who was still there, kicking the ball away to the same field. The only difference was that Jones was now on 150 and on his way to 184 not out. The tactics had clearly not worked.

In 1989, when I was Chairman of Selectors, we were playing Australia and getting a bit of a hiding. Nick Cook was brought into the team for the fourth Test at Old Trafford. He bowled pretty moderately in that match, but in selection we felt that it was unfair on him to be given just the one game. It was not only that, because the Test was played in a dreadful atmosphere. The announcement had been made about the players who were going to South Africa, there was suspicion and worry and there were different groups huddled in different parts of the dressing-room. Furthermore, we had played appallingly badly, and so Nick was chosen again for the next Test at Trent Bridge.

I had already had a word or two with Micky Stewart on this subject of silly fields. His answer was to the effect that the game goes through fashions and this was the current vogue. He said that it was hard to insist on something to a captain or a bowler who believes that the game has moved on and that the current thinking is better than what went before. I kept plugging away on the subject, begging Micky just to give it a try as an alternative. I merely wanted to see if it would work. If it did, fine; if not it would not have been the end of the world, and we could go back to the modern way.

At Trent Bridge, Australian openers Geoff Marsh and Mark Taylor had put on 301 for the first wicket by the close of the first day. With our morale at the lowest possible ebb, I made a further request that we might try what could be termed the old-fashioned way, even if only to prove me wrong. After about an hour's play on the second day, Nick Cook was called up to bowl. Miracle of miracles, there was no silly mid-off and no silly mid-on. There was a slip, four or five in the covers, with one set back, just like the old days. What happened? Cook, nice and relaxed, bowled it slowly and Geoff Marsh, a rather wooden batsman, found it difficult to cope. He had stiff forearms which, against a slow bowler, would not work particularly well. Instead of playing with soft hands, he pushed out at the first four deliveries without knowing quite where they were. He blocked them, but you could see a doubt going through his mind. How could he score runs if the ball was coming on so slowly?

Marsh's answer was to attack. He had a big swish, the ball lobbed off the edge to slip where Ian Botham took the catch. David Boon came in to join Mark Taylor, with the pair of them struggling against an excellent spell of spin bowling. I was chortling away to myself, having my theory proved correct. I did not go into the dressing-room during lunch, but when the players returned to the field after the interval, I could not believe my eyes. Nick Cook was still bowling, but to a field which included a silly mid-off and silly mid-on.

He still bowled well, gaining the notice of *Wisden* which credited him with having 'rediscovered the flight and control that had deserted him in the previous Test'. He had both Taylor and Boon stumped to finish with figures of 40-10-91-3 out of a total of 602 for 6 declared. One wonders what his figures might have been if he had persisted with the same method of attack. As it was, it was the end of the flight and, sadly, the end of Nick Cook at Test level. He played in the next Test at The Oval, but failed to take a single wicket and did not play for England again.

Going back earlier in my career, Robin Marlar was captain of Sussex when I made my début for the county. As captain, he always felt under pressure whenever the ball turned because he was expected to bowl out the opposition. He would tend to bowl flat and quickly in such circumstances. It was a team delegation which went to him to persuade him to look at some film of himself bowling in a previous game when it was perfectly clear that he was rushing up and bowling too fast. He claimed that every time he bowled slowly he was hit for six, but it was explained to him that they would not be able to hit every one for six. If he started with a man out for the catch, it became an entirely different game. As it was, he was bowling four or five quick overs before tossing one up when, without the properly set field, of course it was likely to be hit over the top.

He went into the net and tried to bowl slowly. We implored him to bowl even slower and before long he was able to deliver the ball at a far more appropriate speed without any trouble. The next game was against Leicestershire at Hove on a beautiful flat pitch under a sunny, cloudless sky. He took eleven wickets in the match and nobody ever knew where the ball was going to pitch. Classical slow bowling, with wickets falling where they should for an off-spinner: caught slip, caught short-leg, bowled through the gate, LBW having misjudged the length.

It is a subject which returns to get me excited every time I see a slow bowler firing in his darts with the close fielders waiting for the bat/pad chance. I long for the orthodox approach of, for example, a Bishan Bedi, bowling slowly with some spin. It is always said that, if a batsman is forced to look up above his eye line, he will be in trouble. It is a piece of wisdom passed down from generation to generation and is known to everyone. The problem is nobody pays it any heed. If only a modern spinner would adopt this style of bowling, I know he would be spectacularly successful. It always did work and, nowadays, the batsmen do not get any practice against such a bowler. For someone not to try it is plain silly.

The Exquisite Timing of 'The Kipper'

Colin Cowdrey could be said to be the exact opposite of Peter May. An affable, outgoing, courteous Colin Cowdrey was always ready for a chat and a joke. He had a divine sense of timing, as seen in his ability as a racquets player. I saw him play that game and he showed a wonderful sense of timing with his gentle forearm play and had a wonderful economy of movement. In almost any ball game, timing was his trademark and he was certainly capable of doing almost anything he liked with the bat. That was one side of his character. He was also capable of falling into a rather broody mood during which he could get stuck in a defensive mould. He found great difficulty in getting out of it.

I like to take a little credit for one of his outstanding pieces of batting. In my opinion, he never batted better than in the West Indies when he took over the captaincy from the sick Peter May. While Peter was still there, Colin was dragooned into opening the batting, which was not his regular place at that time. He had to take on the pacemen right from the start, and I saw him do pretty well in the first match in Barbados on a lifting pitch. He was very capable of hanging around, based on his ability to leave the ball, and was a fine judge of a run. He did not run particularly quickly, but he was a good mover.

He was always known as 'The Kipper' because of a tendency to spend any spare time sleeping. He found that if he came out with us for a game of golf on the rest day of a Test Match, he would get back, feel ravenously hungry, and tuck into a big meal. Being well to the comfortable side of the weight spectrum, he found it more beneficial to his waistline to stay in bed rather than doing anything more energetic.

He did not do as well in Trinidad as he had in Barbados, but was magnificent with innings of 114 and 97 in Jamaica. He took over the captaincy in Georgetown, with 65 in the first innings, and by the time we returned to Trinidad for the final Test, the West Indies had added Charlie Griffith to their already formidable attack. We batted together on the first morning for a while, doing little more than survive until lunch. That gave us the chance to consider our strategy. I suggested that we should try to retaliate a bit, otherwise we were going to be 'Aunt Sally's for the attack to batter'. Colin just nodded, without really responding, as we walked out after the interval.

I was certainly in an aggressive mood and was pleased to get my 76, but Colin just picked them off with consummate ease to speed to 119. He picked them off his legs, cut and drove and hooked, displaying all the skills associated with playing quick bowling. He had shown all those qualities during his two innings at Sabina Park. I had gone for an early hook there off Wes Hall and found that the pitch was far too fast for me. He, on the other hand, hooked magnificently and that took a lot of doing with so much pace on the ball.

Colin did play quick bowling exceptionally well,

which was why he was selected to fly out to Australia to join the 1974–75 tour. England's batsmen were undergoing a torrid examination by Lillee and Thomson that had resulted in Dennis Amiss and John Edrich sustaining hand fractures in the first Test. Just coming up to forty-three, Colin Cowdrey arrived in time to play on the fastest pitch in the world in Perth. He went in first wicket down and, finding himself at the non-striker's end with a fired up Jeff Thomson waiting to bowl, is reported to have said in unconcerned tones, 'Hello, I don't believe we've been introduced. My name's Cowdrey.' If Thomson was not rendered speechless, his reply has not been recorded for posterity.

I have only seen what I regarded as the Cowdrey trademark in one other player. You might perhaps be surprised when I identify him as Mark Lathwell of Somerset. Cowdrey would go for the cover-drive, played with a minimum of effort so that cover-point looked as if he could just trot round to pick it up, but suddenly the ball would be racing past cover, apparently accelerating as it went to the boundary with the fielder in absolutely hopeless pursuit. It was this business of the exquisite timing. Sobers, Clive Lloyd, Colin Milburn all sent the ball crashing through the covers, but you could see the effort they had put into their shots.

The reason I liken Lathwell to Cowdrey is that I saw him make 175 for England 'A' against Tasmania in 1993. He hit twenty-five fours in that innings, despite the fact that the outfield was long and others found difficulty in reaching the boundary. He was just stroking the ball

COLIN COWDREY: *He was supreme in his ability to dispatch the ball from his presence with a languid flow of the bat.*

and it kept going, so the muzzle velocity was there even if he made no apparent effort. It was a source of great disappointment to me that he did not come through as I had hoped. In the 1995 season I saw him on television and was moved to send him a little note. I said I was heart-broken to see him shuffling around at the crease and moving his feet before the bowler had let go, breaking all the rules of batting. I did not get a reply, which was rather sad, but perhaps he did not receive my letter.

It is quite something for me even to mention Mark Lathwell in the same context as Colin Cowdrey. Cowdrey was supreme in his ability to dispatch the ball from his presence with a languid flow of the bat. There was no flashy wrist movement, for all the power came, unseen, from his forearm strength. The same economy of movement I had seen on the racquets court was evident in his batting. As he played a stroke with that exquisite timing, The Kipper would leave fielders floundering.

The Edriches

Both Bill and John Edrich were wonderful Test cricketers. You would recognise them as coming from the same Norfolk family stock by their down-to-earth attitude to the game, and yet here were two completely different characters. There was Bill, the wartime bomber pilot who had a go at the game in every sense. Not only was he a highly successful batsman and accomplished slip fielder, but he also opened the bowling for England. One of my first memories of cricket was sitting on the grass at Lord's in 1947 seeing Bill Edrich knocking Dudley Nourse's middle stump out of the ground. It was a good match for Bill. In South Africa's first innings he merely held one catch, but in the second innings he clean bowled three of their top four batsmen, caught the other one along with two more, and scored the matter of 189 as he and Denis Compton put on 370 for the third wicket.

Bill was noted as an on-side batsman with a strong bottom hand and had a well-merited reputation as a fearless puller of the fast bowlers. In his later days he came out to bat in a charity match when Alan Moss was captain of the opposing side. As a Middlesex player himself, Moss knew Bill's batting well, so he put all nine fielders on the leg side for the first ball. Bill went to push it for his single off the mark into the vacant off side, got an inside edge, and was caught at mid-wicket.

Bill was a cavalier in cricket and in life. On one

of my first trips to the Scarborough Festival I found myself sitting with him at dinner. Trying to pick up a

BILL AND JOHN EDRICH: You would recognise them as coming from the same Norfolk family stock ... yet here were two completely different characters.

few pointers to the game, I asked him if he had any tips about playing fast bowling. He turned to me and asked, 'Have you ever been hit in the head by the ball?' 'No, Mr Edrich,' I replied. 'Doesn't hurt a bit,' was all he volunteered in answer to my quest for knowledge.

I would not have got the same response from his cousin John Edrich in later years. John was left-handed and was usually a batsman who just worked the ball around and who played entirely within his limitations. He realised that Test cricket was all about batting a long time and not just a matter of a quick fifty here and there. Occupation of the crease was his objective and he was very good at it. For an opening batsman who was not particularly nimble on his feet, he was a fine player of slow bowling. He was patient and waited without trying to do too much.

If Bill was brave, John was no less so in an era when there was plenty of fast bowling. He took a few real cracks, not least one which was the worst I ever witnessed on a cricket field. Peter Pollock of South Africa was a genuinely quick and nasty bowler, and he felled John Edrich with a ball at Lord's in 1965. Without helmets in those days, John seemed just to freeze against a bouncer and the ball hit him straight between the eyes. The ball did not bounce anywhere, but simply fell to the ground. After a moment when he stood there like a boxer who has just stopped a clean punch, John followed the ball to the ground in a crumpled heap.

There was another side to John Edrich's batting skills. I was in hospital at one point in 1956 recovering from a broken leg sustained in a ridiculous accident with my own car. What made it worse was that I was forced to watch the third Test against New Zealand at Headingley on television instead of playing in it. In the previous Test at Lord's I had scored 62 and 80 not out to help England to victory with only fifteen minutes to spare. Five hours had been lost to rain during the last two days, so we needed 152 to win in just under three hours. I was pleased with my innings which had helped us home with so little time in hand. Ken Barrington, dropped after the first Test for scoring too slowly, was recalled in my place for the third match, while John Edrich was brought in for the injured Geoff Boycott.

John, usually a somewhat dour and unadventurous

batsman, flayed the New Zealand attack to all parts with sparkling strokeplay that could not have been bettered. To be fair, it was not the most penetrative of Test attacks, but he changed gear from his usual rather studied approach to record 310 not out, England's first triple hundred since Hutton's 364 in 1938. Barrington helped himself to 163 as well as the pair put on 369 in 339 minutes. Perhaps John would have stayed longer in this more adventurous mode if he had not been hit by Pollock just a fortnight later. If he had ever heard cousin Bill's observation about getting hit on the head, at that moment he would have realised that it was not entirely accurate.

Bowling to Take Wickets

On reading this heading, you might well ask what other purpose there is in bowling? However, as I now look around the game, some bowlers appear so clueless about dismissing batsmen that you begin to wonder if they really intend to take a wicket as they run in to bowl. There is no doubt that there are some instinctive wicket takers around, not least Dominic Cork, just as there have always been. What concerns me is whether they are present in as great a number as has been the case in the past. Ian Botham would perhaps be the classic example of a wonderful bowler who had a lot going for him anyway, but who was always trying his damnedest to get the batsman out, even if he had 150 to his name and was in total command.

As I grew up as a bowler, I was encouraged to get batsmen out and I was allowed to be inventive as to how I did it. There would be plenty of times when we would say 'Right, we're going to bowl leg-stump to this guy to a leg-side field'. Or, we would aim to bowl straight to a particular batsman, or on the off side to somebody else. It all depended on the way they played. Even at my level of bowling, which was not exactly startling, I do remember having a good match at Adelaide in 1962–63. It was a very, very flat pitch – the sort of conditions when I tended to get plenty of bowling. We bowled a lot of overs in those days and, as the faster bowlers got tired, somebody had to do the work. On this occasion I bowled forty overs in the match, picking up six wickets for 159 which, in the circumstances of Australia scoring 686 in their two innings, was more than respectable.

Much of the time was spent bowling to Bobby Simpson and Brian Booth. Bobby was extremely skilled at working the ball to the leg side, demanding that you bowled more to the off side, while Brian Booth was the other way round. He could get the ball from pretty close to his off-stump through the covers with fine timing and placement. Once they had settled in, I found myself having to bowl to two completely different fields and two completely different lines. To Simpson I kept the ball three or four inches outside off-stump with an off-side field which gave him no opportunity to chip me through mid-wicket or work me to leg. To Booth I kept a tight leg-stump line with perhaps a six-three leg-side field. Not only did I do what I regarded as a pretty good containing job, but I also got both of them out in the second innings. Booth was caught at the wicket down the leg side, and Simpson caught behind down the off side. I was captain so did not have to argue my case, but it was anyway an accepted strategy at the time.

That is not the case today. There have been policies which appear to have undermined what I regard as a very sensible and logical way of bowling to particular batsmen. I have to admit to being a part of the trend when one-day cricket was introduced in this country in the form of the Gillette Cup in 1963. I found myself laying down the law to my bowlers. I insisted that they bowled to hit the stumps. If a ball was going to hit the stumps, it was a good delivery. If it was missing to either side of the wicket or passing over the top, it was a bad ball. If they bowled at the stumps, I would set the field depending on the way in which the batsman played. It might be a six-three field or a five-four, some fielders would be set a little straighter or deeper, all decided by the method of the batsman. I did not want the bowling to be a variable in the equation. We were not trying to get the batsmen out, merely to stop them scoring. Unfortunately, that thinking appears to have carried over into modern captaincy and into the way bowlers think. It is one of the most disastrous consequences of limited-overs cricket for the conventional English game.

I did not disagree with much that Micky Stewart did during his time as manager of the English Test team, but there was one policy which disturbed me greatly. There was much talk of the 'corridor of uncertainty'. This involved bowling three or four inches outside off-stump, close enough to get the batsman to play the ball, but not so wide as to allow him room to play his shots. The field would then be set accordingly. However, if that is the only way you are going to bowl, however the batsman plays and whoever comes in, the bowler stops thinking and he will never develop that essential instinct for taking wickets. In my mind telling the bowler to deliver the ball like a robot with the captain setting the field is no recipe for top-class bowling.

Looking at the current England side, the bowler who seems to be the most pro-active in what he is doing and where he bowls to particular batsmen with special fields is Dominic Cork. He appears to be much more positive than the others about what he wants done, despite the fact that he is not more senior or experienced than his colleagues. He will work away to the good players on a length, and then, to the slightly less able batsmen, he will break it up with more short balls, or yorkers, generally displaying thinking bowling. It works.

England could have done with this sort of cerebral bowling when faced with an opponent like Viv Richards. I was not involved with England at the time, but time and time again I would watch and see a batsman who was hugely strong and who wanted to dominate. To the ball pitching on off-stump or just outside, so hitting middle and leg, he could get a lot of bat on it and send it through mid-wicket. It was his stock in trade. Amazingly, England's field placings would still be set with only the one mid-wicket. Mid-wicket has always been a position of limited value, in that it is impossible to cover as much ground as is required. In the covers it is possible to anticipate a bit by the angle the bat is making. At mid-wicket there are few clues to where the ball is going and it has only got to be beating you by a few yards and the ball is through. You also tend to be a little too close because you are trying to stop the dabbed single off the legs.

Viv Richards would go in and, in no time at all, he would have four or five boundaries through the mid-wicket area. The captain and bowlers would talk and the plan became clear. They would keep the ball right away from the stumps on the off side. Then it was

VIV RICHARDS: A batsman who was hugely strong and who wanted to dominate.

mayhem. He was just as good an off-side player and once the ball was out there, he was no longer taking any risks. Playing off the stumps represented a little bit of a chance, and later in his career, when his reactions were not quite as quick, he did get himself out a few times playing right round his leg, missing it and falling LBW. Back at his peak, somebody should at least have tried putting three men in the mid-wicket area, one for the catch, and two more back a bit to stop the fours. Now, playing the same shot, he would have initially to make sure he has kept it down to avoid being caught. Furthermore, he is now taking the risk for one run instead of four, and he might well decide that the game has not become much fun. Still wanting to dominate, he might attempt to hit the straight ball on to the off side. He was eminently capable of doing that but, early in a Test innings, he would not have necessarily chosen to play that way and might not have been successful even if he tried. At least it would have made him think. As it was, there was a player who dominated at will and whom England completely failed to work out. Get him out early and you save yourself a lot of trouble.

There was another case in point in the England v. Pakistan series in 1992. England won at Headingley by the tensest of margins when Mark Ramprakash joined David Gower to see them to a target of 99 with four wickets down. It was a typically difficult Headingley pitch with the ball seaming and going through at different heights. Only one Pakistani managed to get runs, and he did so in both innings. Salim Malik, who scored 82 not out in the first innings and 84 not out in the second, is as good a cover-driver of the ball as you will ever see, and he hit it just as well on the rise even on that pitch where the ball was misbehaving. He is not nearly as strong off his legs, yet we continued to bowl down the famous corridor of uncertainty. The difference was that, to Malik, it became the corridor of certainty. Anything of a suitable length was certain to be driven through the covers. That gave him plenty of scoring opportunities in a low-scoring game.

The situation cried out for another man on the leg side and for the bowling to be straighter. Then there would have been the option of bowling him or having him LBW. I can remember having a bit of a grouse at Graham Gooch, whose answer was that if the bowlers had been good enough, it might have been different. It might be a bit hard on the bowlers, but the corridor into which they were trying to bowl was some eight to ten inches wide. I would expect most of my generation of Test bowlers to be satisfied with a corridor no wider than four inches. We talked about being able to hit one stump, not just about bowling at the wicket. Brian Statham's warm-up was to go out and bowl at three stumps, knock each one out of the ground and come back having taken only a few balls to achieve the objective. Some modern bowlers would be completely worn out by the time they had hit the last stump and too tired to bowl in the match!

I remember, in my early days as Chairman of Selectors, watching a trial game at Lord's. David 'Syd' Lawrence from Gloucestershire was on view, bowling away in his usual whole-hearted fashion. I usually had to have the odd word with players from time to time, even if I got a bit shy of doing so later on. After seeing him bowl a couple of overs I thought I would count to see how many balls he bowled would hit the stumps. The answer was none. In two whole sessions not one ball would have hit the stumps. I explained that he was expending an awful lot of energy without being able to get a single dismissal bowled or LBW. He just shrugged his shoulders and gave a vague promise to try to do better.

He is not alone among fast bowlers in particular in being wasteful. If they are not bowling to hit the stumps, they must have a wonderful radar which tells them where they are bowling. It must be desperately difficult to bowl any sort of consistent line. I know one always tends to talk of the best, but someone like Malcolm Marshall is able to look back on a high percentage of bowled and LBWs among his victims. It helped not being as tall as some others, the ball staying down at stump height more often, but he was a stump hitter.

Michael Holding, on the other hand, would not have hit the stumps as often, although he did have that wonderful performance at The Oval in 1976 when twelve of his fourteen wickets were either bowled or LBW. That was on a pitch offering so little by way of bounce that the ball skidded through at stump height. In general, however, he just hated being driven and so his natural length became a little shorter, resulting in the ball often passing over the stumps. If he had pitched it up just a little further he might have taken another hundred wickets.

So how do bowlers take wickets? The captain has to give the bowler free rein as to what he wants to do. That can only be discovered by talking to him and asking where he wants his field to achieve his objectives. Only on very rare occasions should the captain modify what the bowler wants to do or, at least, try to argue him round to a different point of view. However it is arrived

MALCOLM MARSHALL: He is able to look back on a high percentage of bowled and LBWs among his victims . . . a thinking bowler.

at, bowling differently to different batsmen must be a prime element of the bowler's art and every time that is eroded, either by one-day cricket or a captain's whim, cricket suffers. It is not only captains having their say; perhaps managers are becoming increasingly influential in disrupting the equilibrium between captain and bowler. The bowler has a hard enough job to do without being told how to bowl or where to bowl it, and the automaton is not the answer. A thinking bowler and a sympathetic captain is the combination which should bring success.

The Complete Cricketer

~

There is only one player in recent times who can aspire to the title of The Complete Cricketer – Sir Garfield St Aubrun Sobers, to give him his full handle or, to cricketers who admired his marvellous talent all over the world, simply Gary. An extraordinary cricketer in the true sense of the word, but also a fine human being. The two things do not always go together, but Gary is a man of great charm with a natural quietness and dignity.

It is a pity that he has not found a way of conveying his brilliant and complete understanding of the game to following generations. It would have been wonderful to see him as a coach, manager, mentor or whatever. On the other hand, he is quite a private man and perhaps he does not give of himself too readily. He can feel a little awkward in company that he does not know, but that is not the case when he is at his best, on his own island of Barbados. There, everybody knows and loves him.

Gary and I have been good personal friends for a long period, and my best times with him have certainly been in Barbados. I have fond memories of an early breakfast on flying fish and lovely fruit, and then, in winter, going to the betting shop and catching the English National Hunt racing. On one occasion, I found that our fellow punters knew a great deal about a horse which I happened to own, called Ocean Diamond. They knew the form backwards and certainly had a greater knowledge of the animal than I had. From the betting shop, there might be a quick call at the tourist board, just to say hello to everyone, and then straight to Sandy Lane for eighteen holes of golf.

Had it not been for cricket, the name of Gary Sobers would probably have been revered in golfing circles just as it is now in cricket. He loves the game and is a very fine player. For a short period he was a little wild in his play, but always hit a long ball with a lovely, lazy swing. He is also very accomplished around the greens, but his putting sometimes lets him down. He can be all right from time to time, but it would not be rated as one of the stronger aspects of his otherwise excellent game. After golf, he likes nothing more than to sit around and have a couple of beers or a Scotch, which is really his tipple. If not talking golf or cricket, his favourite subject is boxing. He is a devotee of the sport and knows all the characters. He loves holding forth on the subject.

While playing, he did not sleep a great deal. He was not one to go out carousing, but he enjoyed sitting around having a few drinks quietly with friends. While not seeking out the wild nightlife, he was not an early to bed man either. After a late night session, he would turn out next morning, if not exactly fresh, still with plenty of energy for whatever was necessary during the day.

Gary Sobers is a sportsman of the highest order, and a pleasant personality who has never done a mean thing on the cricket field. To do so would have been foreign to his nature. I always enjoyed the battles I had with him.

I bowled to him quite a lot, without ever being able to claim his wicket in a Test. I often thought I was going to get him as I could swing the ball in to the left-hander and he favoured playing off the back foot. I would even think I finally had him, but then, at the very last second, he would get half a bat on it, send the ball down to fine leg and give me a huge grin as he ran up the wicket.

Undoubtedly he was the prince among batsmen, and would still rate as the best I ever saw. Why? Because he had no apparent weakness. He never had any trouble against pace, to the extent that I never saw him duck a ball. At the same time, I never saw him get hit, even on the body, let alone the head. He was a wonderful hooker because he had this terrific high backlift and played very late off the back foot. In fact, he really only came forward to drive. He was a beautiful player of spin bowling, too. He played it off the pitch, but could still sweep into a drive when the ball was there to be driven. Of course, if the spinner dropped anything short, he would murder it.

Medium-pacers, like myself, always thought we might have a chance to undo him, but that was not the case. I remember Tom Cartwright, one of the finest exponents of the medium-pacer's craft, being asked who played him best. It was in a batting seminar, and I was terrified that he was going to quote a forward player who could nullify his swing through the air and cut off the pitch. Without hesitation he said, 'Gary Sobers, simply because I could never get him to come forward.'

He was also a wonderfully straight player. With his

GARY SOBERS: The image of him with the bat going right through the arc and down his back is one that will never be forgotten by anyone who saw it.

great, high backlift, the bat was absolutely perpendicular in defence and in exactly the same plane when he swung it through. The image of Sobers with the bat going right through the arc and down his back is one that will never be forgotten by anyone who saw it. It was a magnificent sight, particularly as it was achieved with such grace of movement and was never reliant on raw power. He was the complete batsman who could vary his game according to the situation. He would not even need to think about it; he just knew what was required. He could hit six sixes in an over, as he did at Swansea in 1968, or just as easily play out maiden over after maiden over if that was what was needed.

What of his bowling? He began as an orthodox left-arm spinner, without being anything too special, perhaps. He developed that to bowl a bit of wrist spin, which he did very nicely. He could bowl both the chinaman and the googly, but did not bowl very much in that style. It was not long before he began to develop his medium-quick style, and there we saw something quite extraordinary. He had a wonderful action with a tremendous turn in the gather so that he was really looking over his right shoulder at the target. Then came an easy whip of the body, producing considerable pace from no more than an amble in to the wicket. He was fast enough to bowl an effective bouncer, noted for its accuracy. He also produced fluent inswing from the turn of his body, but could cut the ball away just as well.

From a fairly slow start as a bowler in Test cricket he became a considerable force. Even when his knees began to give way, he would still bowl over after over for not very many runs. For instance, on his last tour to England in 1973 his knees had virtually gone, but he was still an essential part of the attack. The following winter, England went to the Caribbean and he played in four of the five Tests, bowling over 220 overs and took fourteen

wickets in the series. That takes a bit of doing, wh[...]
is bowling, and particularly by somebody so far [...]
full fitness.

As a fielder, he was perhaps not a very fast mover over a long distance, but he was extremely quick to the ball over a short one with a very acceptable arm. As a close catcher he was quite outstanding. In those days, when he fielded at short-leg, he would just move in quietly until he could almost pick the ball off the bat. As a captain, he might have been too nice-natured to be the consummate leader. There was nothing wrong with his captaincy, even when he made the famous declaration against England at Port-of-Spain in 1968. Fooled into thinking that his back-up bowlers could do the job when Charlie Griffith was injured, he set England 215 to win in two and three-quarter hours. England won by seven wickets with three minutes to spare, so it was not an outrageous declaration, but it cast something of a cloud over his captaincy. It was said that, from then on, customs officials on islands other than Barbados would delight in asking him if he had anything to declare.

He was a very fair opponent and it was a pleasure to play against Gary when he was captain. That is not to say he was a soft touch. He could run the show merely by his own play. He did not necessarily have to be the best man-manager in the business because if things were going wrong he could usually turn them around himself.

Perhaps his finest hours came after he had played league cricket, county cricket, domestic cricket in the West Indies, and Test cricket. He then played Sheffield

Shield cricket in Australia, helping South Australia to win the competition for the first time in eleven years. Before the last match that season, against Victoria, he had said at the team meeting that they should not worry, just leave the bowling to him. He also said that they could leave the batting to him as well, and he did not let them down. Nine wickets in the match, an innings of 124, plus four catches. He completed the double of a thousand runs and fifty wickets in that Australian season, with six centuries.

No doubt at the end of the match he sat back with a beer enjoying the company of his fellow players. He would have told his tales, punctuated by the warmest and most infectious of chuckles, gradually developing into a torrent of raucous laughter. As the evening went on, the accent would have deepened into almost impenetrable Bajan. His team-mates might not have understood a word he said at that point, but they would have laughed along with the most accomplished player with whom they ever shared a dressing-room. He is that type of person. You are never likely to be miserable in the company of Sir Garfield St Aubrun Sobers – The Complete Cricketer.

With Thanks from Dennis Lillee

I played against Australia in England in 1968. I had officially retired in 1965 but was called back by Colin Cowdrey in the face of a growing injury crisis. In fact Colin himself had to miss the fourth Test that summer, allowing Tom Graveney to add his name to the list of England captains in an Ashes series. Coincidentally, the Australian captain Bill Lawry was also injured, so Tom tossed the coin with another stand-in skipper, Barry Jarman.

It was an extraordinary series, in that England were represented by no fewer than seven men who had been or would be captain of their country. I played at Headingley in the fourth Test and stayed in the team which went to The Oval for the final match when we squared the series at one-all with just five minutes to spare. Derek Underwood took seven second innings wickets after a freak storm at lunch on the final day had flooded the outfield and play was only possible because the crowd helped the groundstaff in mopping-up operations.

Graham McKenzie was the fastest bowler Australia had and, although he could be nippy with a good bouncer, he was not a real physical threat. Alan Connolly was their other opening bowler. He was a comfortable proposition to face as far as speed was concerned, even though he did bowl me with a good one which moved off the pitch at Headingley and bowled me again at The Oval. In general, that pair lacked real pace and were not brimming over with aggression. It was not too bad a series in which to make a comeback, and far better than it would have been in 1970–71 on Ray Illingworth's tour to Australia when I caught my first glimpse of Dennis Lillee.

Lillee had gathered something of a reputation as a young man as a tearaway with plenty of pace, and displaying the aggression which had been missing from the Australian attack in 1968. England had enjoyed the better of the first two Tests without being able to force a win. Melbourne had been a total wash-out, but England had gone one up by a crushing 299-run margin in Sydney. The teams returned to Melbourne for a hastily re-arranged Test which ended in a draw, and so Australia were under some pressure when they went to Adelaide for the next match, one down with two to play.

Having lost in Sydney, the Australian selectors panicked. It is reassuring to know that they can make mistakes as well, because they dropped Graham McKenzie and Alan Connolly, replacing them with Alan 'Froggy' Thomson and Ross Duncan. It was Duncan's only Test appearance, for he failed to take a wicket, and for the next Test in Adelaide, they introduced Dennis Keith Lillee to the side. He was sharp if not outstandingly quick, he sprayed it around a little, but he displayed enough aggression to grab himself a five-wicket haul in England's first innings. Even so, his pace was not remarkable and, good athlete though he was, he had not yet achieved the real spring and elasticity of some who come to mind. What he had got was the makings of a first-class action with nothing vital missing. The run-up was smooth and purposeful, he had a prodigious leap into the gather, he turned into a perfect sideways-on position and, above all, he completed his action with a full shoulder swing. From what one heard of the man's personality, he had this aggressive streak but it was not obvious that he would refine his bowling to make the huge strides and improvement which would take him to the very pinnacle of his trade.

He went through various stages in his career. There was that tearaway stage. There was the refinement with a reduction in the run-up and a slightly more studied approach to his bowling. There was the injury period when he suffered a crippling back problem which meant that he had to work hard to return himself to Test fitness. Then there was the final fruition when he learned all the arts and crafts of the fast bowler with swing, cut, change of pace and always wonderfully high-armed to get the ball to deviate.

As for general pace, he always sustained that well enough, but there is no doubt that he enjoyed the benefits of bowling in tandem with Jeff Thomson. While batsmen were ducking and weaving in self-preservation against Thommo's extreme pace at one end, they then had to deal with the immaculate accuracy and movement of Lillee at the other. The greatest evidence of pace came in Lillee's bouncer, which he was not shy of using. There was plenty of short-pitched stuff, but I always felt that he put so much into his bouncer that his pace came down a

DENNIS LILLEE AND JEFF THOMSON: While batsmen were ducking and weaving in self-preservation against Thommo's extreme pace at one end, they then had to deal with the immaculate accuracy and movement of Lillee at the other.

bit when he was bowling to a fuller length.

I can even remember comparing the emerging Dennis Lillee with the not so long retired Freddie Trueman. I have never been persuaded to change my mind from feeling that Fred, in his pomp, actually generated more pace and hit the 'keeper's gloves just that little bit harder.

The bouncer, however, was different again. It was a very useful Lillee weapon and, of course, he directed it so well that he did not waste many. Lillee grew up under the captaincy of Ian Chappell and it was a period of Australian cricket which I did not particularly admire. It seemed that they had decided to be more typically Australian than the most extreme caricature of Australians, to the extent that they could be really rather boorish in their nationalism. The only way you could prove that you were a proper member of the team, one hundred per cent committed, was to show your feelings in an extreme way whether that meant crashing into the dressing-room and throwing your bat around when you were out, or drinking more beer than the next bloke in the evening.

When they came over to England in 1972, I had not been long out of the game and remembered the splendid hospitality I had always enjoyed when visiting Australia, so I felt it was only right to try to repay that. I had a motor boat down on the Solent at that time and a few of them came down to enjoy a day out. They did, however, stick pretty close together and there was not a lot of obvious relish or thanks for what I was providing. I dare say that is true of all young men; they do not find it easy to show their appreciation but I would have been grateful for a semblance of a show of manners. Dennis Lillee was very much a part of that scene, no doubt making him a more effective bowler. It made the batsman see what he was made of and let him know that someone meant business at the other end.

That small amount of entertainment apart, I did not really get to know the Australian players and I might be making a judgement on too little evidence. I spent very little time with Lillee, but the next time they came to England in 1975, with Lillee and Thomson at their peak, I was working for the *Sunday Mirror*. Suddenly we had a bright idea of getting the nightmare photograph of Lillee bowling one side of the wicket and Thomson the other, synchronising their actions so we had the picture of the two of them coming at the camera at the same time. We did that and then thought a good bouncer picture would be fun.

I had never been hit on the head by a bouncer and, as I knew it was coming, I thought I would be able to avoid the ball. At the last minute, we were unable to take the pictures on a first-class ground and we had to go to a club where the pitch was not quite so even. I wondered a little about the prospect, but we got some photographs of Dennis bowling the bouncers wide on the off side and me ducking. At the end of the session I asked the photographer if he had what he wanted. He said that he was unsure of the authenticity, so I suggested that we do a couple for real. Just to show Lillee's control of accuracy, the first one not only pitched in the right place, it seamed back, I had to readjust and it clanged off the side of my head. Concussion was diagnosed for a day or two, but I still have a nice photograph of the two of us smiling together after the incident. It did confirm to me the old Bill Edrich theory that being hit on the head by a cricket ball does not actually hurt. It might not have inflicted pain, but it certainly scrambled my brains a little.

The last time I saw Lillee in action was in 1977 in the Centenary Test at Melbourne. The first two innings were very low scoring affairs. Australia bowled out for 138, England replying with a paltry 95 thanks largely to Dennis Lillee's return of 13.3-2-26-6. I could not believe the difference in the Melbourne pitch from the days when I played there. There were great plates of thick grass and then just flat mud and more thick grass. It looked like a nightmare and played like one, in the first innings at lest.

At the major dinner after the match, I was at the Lillee table and heard some discussion about what was a good pitch and what was not. It was an era when I did not think the pitches, in general, were as good as they had been in the late 1950s and 1960s. I admit that I had enjoyed a couple of glasses of wine but I found myself saying to Lillee, who had taken another five wickets in the second innings, that I doubted whether he had ever bowled on a really flat pitch. Even in 1977, when he was moving on in his career and at a social occasion after a brilliantly successful match, he had lost none of that native aggression which made him the great bowler he was. Having assailed my head in 1975, he now gave me a real earful. On reflection, I probably deserved it.

The Left-Handers' Honeymoon

When the LBW Law was changed in 1972, I could foresee that the game would be taken over by left-handed batsmen. Because most of the bowling was quick and because most of it, some ninety per cent, was right-arm over-the-wicket, any left-hander seemed to have a huge advantage. The normal way for the ball to go is to pitch outside the right-hander's off-stump and come back into the batsman. The same delivery to the left-hander has pitched outside the leg-stump and therefore cannot gain an LBW decision and, as an extension of that, the batsman should not be bowled. Virtually everything hitting the stumps has pitched outside leg, unless it is overpitched when the batsman says 'thank you very much' for the half-volley.

Nothing has happened since to change my view and there are several successful left-handers about, including the most exciting batsman in the world. I am sure that if Brian Lara were right-handed, he would not have the same freedom to score at the pace he does because the ball would be coming at a different angle. The fact that a lot of left-handers are not as successful as they might be is always put down to that question of angle. We are told that they have to deal with the awkward problem of the ball going across them. To me that appears to be a red herring. It is only going across left-handers at a difficult angle if they choose to make it so.

The left-handed batsmen who stand in such a way that

BRIAN LARA: The most exciting batsman in the world.

they play the ball back towards the bowler or on the leg side does not have a problem. The only ball which the batsman encounters going across him at a difficult angle is the one which would probably be missing another set of stumps outside the off-stump which he tries to play towards extra-cover. That is the key to Graham

Thorpe's under-achievement in the early days of his Test career, for he sees extra-cover as a profitable place to get runs. David Gower sometimes fell into the same trap, but he tended to play later and with a cleaner swing of the bat and so got away with it more. When Graham Thorpe plays shots into that area, there is not much of the face of the bat offered to the ball. He would be better off swinging the bat through rather than playing an inside-out checked drive.

The great exponent of playing the ball so that it was not going across him was Bill Lawry, the Australian left-handed opener. He did play and miss plenty, but he was very good at lining the ball up. He did not appear to have a great natural talent but was enormously successful because he simply never tried to hit the ball towards extra-cover. If the ball was widish he either left it alone or hit it straight by getting across to it, or he dropped it down on the off side and ran. If other left-handers were to think more like Lawry, they could reassess their angles and be very much more successful.

I always said that I wished I could have been in the left-handers' place by having a vast majority of the bowling I faced as left-arm over-the-wicket. In fact I once had a bet with an old Cambridge friend, Ian McLachlan, who had a distinguished career with South Australia. Before the 1962–63 tour he said that we would have serious problems with Australia's left-arm seamer Alan Davidson. I made the bold statement, backed by hard cash, that he would not get me out more than once in the series. I was caught by Bobby Simpson off

ALAN DAVIDSON: I made the bold statement, backed by hard cash, that he would not get me out more than once in the series.

Davidson's bowling in the second innings of the third Test in Sydney, but I won my bet as that was the only time in the series that he claimed my wicket.

What I liked about facing the left-armer was that the chances of his hitting the stumps were remote, providing he failed to swing it into me. All there was to worry about was the angle. If the ball was overpitched, I felt I had all the freedom in the world to hit it. If it pitched short, I could go for the pull with impunity because, having pitched outside leg, there was no danger of being LBW.

The one difficulty that the left-handed batsman does have which is not self-imposed is the rough outside his off-stump when facing a spinner. However, there are not that many spinners around to make use of the rough. Most of the bowling is still quick and right-arm-over. Bowlers do tend to come round the wicket more to left-handers nowadays, but they are seldom using the rough because they tend to bowl at the stumps. On balance, the left-handers enjoy a permanent honeymoon.

Ducking the Issue

~

It is often said that there is nothing new in cricket. Even the four-pronged pace attack, so often described as a West Indian innovation, was not new in 1979. Twenty years earlier, at Melbourne, I played against an Australian side which included Davidson and Lindwall as the new ball bowlers, followed by Meckiff and Rorke who took over once the shine had gone. As there were serious questions asked about the legality of the actions of the last pair who, furthermore, used drag so effectively that they were often delivering from no more than eighteen yards away, it was a very formidable attack.

There was, however, an essential difference in 1959 in that the long slow, walk back had not been developed as a means of wasting time, as became usual for the West Indians. I do not think this was planned as a cynical strategy, it was more a case of natural selection – the longer the walk back took, the greater time became available to recuperate. Sports science was advancing and fitness now was defined by speed of recovery. Interval training was the vogue so, if the actual run-up was twenty-five yards, a bowler who walked back forty yards and then trotted in for the first fifteen before getting into the run proper had that much more time to recover and stay fresh.

The influence of this on the over rate was absolutely disastrous. There were times when the West Indians got the rate down to no more than seventy-two overs in a day, with sessions of twenty-four overs bowled by four fast bowlers. Each knew that he only had to bowl six overs in each session so he could maintain full pace and aggression throughout the day. Certainly at home, there was no limitation on the bouncer, so suddenly an excellent score in a day batting against the West Indians was under 200 runs. Consider the number of balls available for run-scoring, despite attacking fields, and it just had to be. If teams did not understand what they were up against and still tried to score in the region of 250 or 260 runs, they came a cropper.

The whole nature of the game had changed, especially when involved in a series. The fact was that opponents did not get enough time to score enough runs to beat the West Indies. It was possible to avoid defeat, but not to win. To get enough runs leaving enough time to bowl them out twice, with the over rate down so low, was extremely hard.

Clive Lloyd was the architect of this form of attack, and I would not necessarily blame him. As so often happens, here was a man faced with a choice. He had the fast bowlers, he had the ammunition, and he was a competitive animal. With no legislation to prevent it, most captains would have opted to take advantage of the situation. At the same time, there is no reason to admire his captaincy vastly, hugely successful though it was. I have always imagined that, when this fast bowling quartet failed to take a wicket in a session, the interval discussion went something along the lines of 'Which one of you wants to be selling souvenirs on the beach next

JOEL GARNER AND CURTLEY AMBROSE: The strategy was determined. Only the personnel changed.

month? If you go on bowling like beach-bums, one of you has got to go.' They would come out after the interval bowling like men possessed.

It did not need much imagination, just a case of rotating these high-quality bowlers. When you had the likes of Roberts, Holding, Garner and Croft at your disposal, subtle nuances of captaincy were seldom required. Then Marshall, Clarke, Davis, Baptiste, Daniel, Patterson, Walsh, Ambrose, Benjamin, Bishop and the rest came into the equation and the strategy was determined. Only the personnel changed.

There were, of course, some disgraceful episodes of intimidation that have marred the enjoyment to be had from seeing these wonderful bowlers in operation. One which springs to my mind was an evening at Old Trafford in 1976 when Brian Close and John Edrich were the unfortunate recipients of an all-out physical barrage. Here, again, the whole of the cricketing hierarchy needs to take the blame because the umpires completely failed to take the appropriate action. They could have stepped in but, over the years, they have consistently avoided the issue.

The combination of long intervals between deliveries, and the lack of control of short-pitched bowling, made it virtually impossible for even the best players to counteract. It all went on for a pretty long time. Even with the ninety overs in a day stipulation, fines for slow over rates, and the other legislation brought in to try to stem the tide, nothing effective was really achieved. Allan Border complained, in a series in Australia, that the game had become so physical that it was just a question of self-defence. Boxing, not batting, had always been described as the noble art of self-defence.

The first piece of effective legislation was the one bouncer per over per batsman condition introduced in Test matches. That did seem to have a generally civilising effect on the whole business of fast bowling. It was still an effective weapon, but not the entire armoury, and it was operating within the spirit of the game. There was a move towards greater diversity in selection. It was slight but noticeable. Test matches were still finished and there was a general improvement in the variety of the game. That is what the four fast bowler concept does to cricket which is such a disservice – eliminate the variety which is so much of the game's charm. From both the players' and the spectators' point of view, with four quicks in operation it is difficult to maintain interest and even notice who is bowling. It is either him or him.

I am always surprised that the batsman in the game have not formed a union of their own to try to make sense of this situation. The fact that they have not is because they have to be macho, and however fast and however dangerous the attack, they feel they must be up to it. It is something to be overcome. It is, however, an appalling thought that generations of batsmen might be brought up to see the games in terms of all-out pace, helmets, chest guards, arm guards and the other protective equipment, just developing some sort of strategy whereby they could survive the physical side of the game.

They would believe that batting was only about scoring runs where they could and would miss all the fun of playing against different types of bowling. Apart from being a test of physical courage, batting should be a cerebral test, involving the unravelling of the mysteries of left-arm and leg-spin, countering the wiles of the medium-pacer. Wicket-keepers too have been poorly served by the predominance of pace. Just to stand back like a goalkeeper and take the ball rocketing through is so boring when compared with the art and challenge of standing up to the wicket. It was exciting to see Godfrey Evans standing up to Alec Bedser. There was a time when the wicket-keepers all stood up to the medium-fast bowler. Then they went back where they caught more but stumped fewer.

By the very nature of things, when you are sitting down to selection, the choice of the fourth fast bowler becomes a problem. Perhaps the West Indies did have four quality fast bowlers available, but usually the balance only has to shift a little to justify picking a good spinner rather than an average quick. Perhaps even a slower swing bowler becomes viable to add some variety so that captains can change the bowling, not just change the bowler. While they can get away with sneaking in the ninety overs in about six and a half hours with no more than a little bit of a fine, and so long as the umpires do not intervene when it becomes too physical, then the whole miserable business will go on.

In 1994, for reasons best known to themselves, some countries voted back the two bouncers per over per batsman allowance. How legislators can possibly get themselves into a situation where they sanction the possibility of two-thirds of the balls in a day's play literally whistling over the head of the batsmen, without any come back at all, really does seem utterly ridiculous. In the committees on which I sit, we are working hard to try to get back to a limit of one bouncer per over per batsman and, with the odd variation, we might well get there. It shows that cricket legislation has a long way to go when it comes up with such a daffy way of dealing with a difficult and long-established problem in the game, namely the domination of fast bowlers and the stereotyped way of playing which comes with them.

The Age of the All-Rounder

~

I always wanted to be considered as an all-rounder. Most cricketers who reach the top start life in this category, because natural talent allows them to indulge in both disciplines during their young days, but gradually one facet of their ability takes over and they specialise as either a batsman or a bowler. This can be due to a personal preference, injury or even opportunity.

When I went up to Cambridge I was considered to be an all-rounder. At Fenner's, however, I hardly got the chance to bowl. I could bowl at a decent pace and had a natural away-swing, but to demonstrate it I had to make sure I bowled a lot in the nets, particularly at the captain. He realised that I wanted to bowl and could bowl. Eventually I got the chance and developed as a bowler. I had a return of 5 for 8 for the Gentlemen against the Players, with three more wickets in the second innings which included Denis Compton twice. I was on at the right time on a rain-affected wicket which started to lift a bit.

Bowling constituted an important part of my game. I bowled plenty of overs, especially away from England. I regarded myself as being useful, just hasty enough with a bit of swing in most conditions. Then a leg injury intervened and, without knowing it, I modified my action to take account of the injury and found I had lost it. I kept bowling but was nothing like my former self. That was a great disappointment, because I had taken pride in being an athlete who could compete in all aspects of the game. I wanted not only to bat, but to be able to bowl and catch and throw. It sometimes amuses me to see England bowlers who get fat benefits before retiring from the game after careers during which they got fewer wickets than I have. Perhaps that is a product of the modern format of the game but, for the record, I did take 419 first-class wickets at a cost of under thirty each.

Being an all-rounder can be very demanding. If you have played a long innings and then have to go out and bowl your overs as well, it is great fun but also very hard work. I remember at the end of one season finding that my legs were like lead for the last six weeks. They would barely warm up throughout the day, with hamstrings as tight as violin strings.

Bearing in mind the physical demands on all-rounders, it is perhaps not surprising that not too many emerge. How is it, then, that cricket in the 1980s was character-ised by the simultaneous emergence of four outstanding all-rounders in Imran Khan, Richard Hadlee, Ian Botham and Kapil Dev? Four marvellous cricketers hailing from four different countries in the same era. They were all major players in their teams, but now, a few years on, the international scene is as lacking in all-round ability as it was rich such a relatively short time ago.

It is possible to put forward a few names, but they tend to be way short in quality when compared with those from the immediate past. Perhaps the Australians come nearest to providing a quality all-rounder through

Ian Healy, their wicket-keeper. In the bowler/batsman all-rounder category, Pakistan's Wasim Akram is reasonably competent as an attacking batsman but you would not classify him as a quality batsman in the way of Kapil Dev, Imran Khan or Ian Botham.

England have been trying to find a replacement for Ian Botham ever since he retired, and were even trying to find one before he left. There has been nobody who could lace his boots. Chris Lewis was given a fair chance but then could not even get into the side. Dominic Cork may eventually be up to quality, but has yet to be thoroughly proven. You have to look at Jack Russell, again as a wicket-keeper/batsman, as the nearest there is to a genuine all-rounder among established players.

The West Indies have not been noted over the years as a profitable source of all-rounders, except when they could boast the greatest of them all in Sir Garfield Sobers. India have Manoj Prabhakar who is certainly competent as both a batsman and a bowler, but might have a way to go in terms of pure quality. Brian McMillan of South Africa is another who has to be considered near the top of the class of '95.

There is no doubt that we were extraordinarily privileged to have the great four all playing together. If you were to ask me which of those four I would really like to go and watch, for all the great feats of the other three, I would plump for Kapil Dev as just about my favourite cricketer of modern times. I first saw him at Lord's as just a whippy young lad without any spare flesh. He ran in and went into that wonderfully extravagant gather

KAPIL DEV: He ran in and went into that wonderfully extravagant gather.

and lovely high right arm with the ability to swing the ball away from the bat.

He developed until it was real quality, high-class swing and seam bowling. He knew exactly what he was doing with the ball. He kept himself extremely fit, and was very seldom out of the side for any reason. He went on to amass 434 wickets in Tests and for much of the time was bowling fast on unresponsive Indian pitches. What might he have achieved if he had bowled on English pitches all the time?

The other side to Kapil's cricket was his batting. It was so simple in style as to be refreshing. He just stood up and hit the ball hard with a nice easy swing of the bat. He was always happy to put bat to ball and, a sweet striker, he was able to time the ball from the moment he came in. He was an exciting and exuberant player, worthy of taking his place in the Pantheon reserved by his countrymen for Indian cricketers possessing special qualities.

Imran Khan was an interesting character and a wonderful athlete. He too had a very extravagant action, but it was a bad action. He would jump out sideways and land with his left foot literally parallel to the bowling crease. How he did not break his ankle with this foot position was always a mystery to me. What he did do eventually was to tear all the ligaments in his ankle. It was after this, I believe, that he went away to teach himself to bowl properly with his front foot pointing down the wicket, enabling him to run through and complete his action. In that period he had learned to swing the ball away from the bat and was a quality bowler.

The interesting thing was that it was just in that period that the business of reverse swing first surfaced from Pakistan. Sarfraz Nawaz tends to take the credit of having discovered it, but Imran Khan certainly developed reverse swing within two or three years of finding his best action. I remember, seeing the ball dipping in so quickly, that my first reaction was to bemoan the fact that he had lost his away-swing. Of course, reverse swing in the right hands is a deadly weapon and Imran possessed the ability to use it to its fullest effect. He could make the ball deviate so late that the batsmen found the greatest difficulty in getting a bat on it at all.

As a batsman, Imran was a watchful player who favoured the back foot. He never had any trouble against quick bowling and could adapt his approach to batting according to the situation. He was a good striker when he wanted to be, but could also take his time if required. He was good technically, if of the square-on variety, but he let the ball come up to him and handled the short delivery particularly well. In fact, of the four, I would pick him as the man whose skills were most equally divided because both Kapil Dev and Hadlee definitely come into the category of bowlers who batted, as indeed does Ian Botham.

Richard Hadlee, later Sir Richard, developed his bowling into a well-oiled machine and achieved a then record number of Test wickets. Actually getting the record was a painful process, for he needed one more to overtake Ian Botham as he began the first Test against England in his home town of Christchurch in 1988. I was there as a journalist and watched as Hadlee bowled over after over without taking a wicket. Then he strained a calf muscle and had to retire from the match and the series. Ironically, it was the first time he had broken down in seventy-four Tests.

RICHARD HADLEE: He developed his bowling into a well-oiled machine.

He eventually took his 374th wicket at Bangalore in November 1988, and went on to take his 431st Test wicket with his final ball at Edgbaston in 1990. Even then, he was still a formidable opponent, if not at the height of his powers but not far off. I do not think that the England batsmen, and particularly Michael

Atherton, were given full credit for withstanding the threat posed by Hadlee on that tour. It was quality bowling of the standard which had come to be normal for him. Of course, he bowled a very high number of overs to reach his record, quite simply because for so many years he was the New Zealand no. 1, without serious contenders at no. 2. He had to develop his bowling along the route he did, because he was going to bowl so much that he would not be able to be an out-and-out strike bowler as he was at the start of his career. But what a bowler it made him.

His batting, on the other hand, was something of a hit and miss affair. He was the only one of the four to be a left-hander, and left-handers always get a bit more freedom to hit the ball against the right-arm over-the-wicket bowler. Hadlee had a lot of trouble with the short ball in his early days especially, not knowing how to move laterally to get away from it, and had a reputation of not being a very good player of quick bowling. The helmet probably helped him to watch the ball a little longer and gave him confidence, and he certainly played some important innings for New Zealand. He was a pure striker, without much movement of the feet, but could just pick the ball up on the leg side and swing the bat through on the off side. A good timer and clean hitter, like all those batsmen who do not move around very much, he could strike the ball nicely because he was standing around waiting for it. For the same reason, however, their defence is not as strong as it might be.

IAN BOTHAM: *A wonderfully strong bowler, capable of long spells with his fine action.*

Finally, Ian Botham. His career went through such distinctly different stages. He began in what might be termed the minor Test league when Packer took all the first teams away. He came in to play what was virtually second eleven Test cricket. It has to be admitted that he moved to a hundred wickets in record time with a slightly debased coinage; that is not to say he was not a wonderful bowler, but he was not performing against the world's top batsmen. His second hundred Test wickets were of high quality.

A wonderfully strong bowler, capable of long spells with his fine action and the ability to swing the ball away sharply and, even better, to bring it in sharply to left-handers, against whom he was deadly. Sadly, his growing weight problem crept up on him and while, in one sense, it gave him great strength and made him feel empowered, the elasticity started to wane. Botham failed to look after himself as he might have done, and that probably led to his severe back problems entailing major surgery. This, in turn, heralded a steady decline in his bowling powers, however much he was still to be feared. His appearances for England became more intermittent as injuries occurred and that magical away-swinger disappeared. He could still run the ball away, but not with that sharp, late away-swing that had been his trademark before. His last hundred or so Test wickets began to cost a good deal more and took longer to get.

Nevertheless, it was a superb career. Apart from his wickets, there was wonderful fielding close to the bat, with all the concentration needed to achieve such a quality of catching. Of course, that again was just part of the picture, for added to the wickets and the catches were all the runs that made Ian Botham a genuine all-rounder. There was no question that his batting was powerful, but there was a minimum of correct footwork and his lofted driving tended to be in and out. He liked hooking, but in truth was an indifferent hooker, frequently not looking at the ball but just ducking his head and swinging the bat. Being as strong as he was and with his undoubted ability, he would still make contact from time to time and find the boundary, or far beyond. He was a devil to bowl at once he got in and started to hit, but the West Indians never had too much trouble with him, as is shown by his record against them which was no better than moderate. That was not by chance; he simply did not play them very well.

My own experience of Ian was limited. I do, however, remember going to Worcester to watch Graeme Hick and Tim Curtis batting with a view to a forthcoming Test team. It was at a time when Botham was just coming back from injury and, consequently, I did not really have him in mind for England selection. It was one of those trips which is the bane of selectors, for instead of seeing Worcestershire bat, they were in the field. That left me still waiting to see my batsmen, but there was a bonus in that I saw Botham bowl.

He managed to out-bowl everybody, getting more life out of the pitch and more movement than had hitherto been seen. A great storm blew up, resulting in the players leaving the field and what looked like the end of play for the day, so I set off back towards London. Imagine my horror when I turned on the radio to hear that play had restarted. Furthermore, Ian Botham had actually batted and had been hit on the cheekbone, sustaining a serious injury. All my new plans for selection had gone out of the window.

Later on he did come back into the England side while I was in charge, midway through the 1989 season when Australia were giving us a hiding. It was the first time I had really been close to the man and had the opportunity to find out what he was like in a team. He was a very strong influence on the side. David Gower was captain, but Botham's presence was still very evident. It was not, I felt, always for the best. Aggression was his watchword, and he thought that aggression was all that was required to ensure success. In his case, I am sure that was what carried him through to such great heights, but it does not work that way for everyone. His narrow approach to the game did not particularly endear him to me.

His aggression failed to produce the required results during that series, scoring 62 runs in four knocks while his three wickets cost over 80 apiece. He went out of the side. Next time he came back, against the West Indies in 1991, he was a different character again. It seemed that he had accepted he was near to his swan-song, he could not rule the roost in the way he once had and really played the ideal supportive role as the stock bowler. I felt much more able to approach him. I told him that four or five wickets and 70 or 80 runs and he would have done a good job. 'That'll do for the first innings, Chairman. What about the second?'

In fact he scored 31 in the first innings before going down in the scorebook as 'hit wicket' when, as so memorably described by Brian Johnson and Jonathan Agnew, he failed to get his leg over. He took 1 for 27 off eleven overs and 2 for 40 off sixteen overs, so he was a useful member of the team which won at The Oval. He went on to the World Cup and was quite definitely the architect of the win at Sydney over Australia which allowed England to top their group and go through to the later stages. His great contribution in that match was as a bowler, but he also managed to talk himself into opening the innings which I thought was an absolute disaster that did not work. In that particular match the ploy did come off, but excluding that innings of 53, his contribution with the bat was minimal. It is one thing to stand up and swish away at tiring bowling, but quite another to take the attack to quality bowlers with the new ball, particularly when he was at very much latter stages of his career.

The Enigmatic Peter May

Peter May was my first captain in Test cricket, and his reputation was well established when I first played under him in 1958. He had already had his great partnership with Colin Cowdrey against the West Indian spinners the year before, and was near the height of his powers as a supreme batsman and captain of his country. I found myself batting with him in my first Test innings on a dank day at Old Trafford against New Zealand. Tony MacGibbon, Johnny Hayes and Bob Blair were big raw-boned pace bowlers, the pitch was damp, the light not good and the ball was moving about. Peter May played and missed a few times, and I certainly did. The situation was quite awkward.

I got the impression that he considered me to be something of a young scallywag, and he was probably right, but he offered me plenty of encouragement. He had been very kind and welcoming, as he always was, but I did not yet feel that I knew him very well. Suddenly he walked down the pitch and said, 'There's nothing for it, I think they've got to go.' The next thing I knew the ball was whistling over extra cover and to all parts as he simply took the attack apart.

It was part of the oddity about Peter that here was this quiet and reserved man, yet the moment he got the bat in his hand he was all aggression. During one of his early Tests in the West Indies, he went in and hit his first ball, or certainly one of his first, for six. Len

Hutton, his captain, was batting at the other end, and enquired of him what was going on. Peter replied that he had not quite got to it so thought he ought to carry on through with the shot. A power and tension was present in his batting which was not obvious in his normal demeanour.

I remember seeing him flogging Roy Gilchrist all round the Scarborough ground when the West Indian was himself being aggressive, as he was fast enough to be. Admittedly it was an easy-paced pitch, but he still hit him high, wide, and handsome, on to the top of the pavilion and all around the ground, in a most dominating piece of batting.

I was reminded of the real quality of his play when he made a few comeback appearances after receiving treatment for cancer of the bowel which had first manifested itself when he had to return from a tour to the West Indies in 1960. He still played, but by 1963 played in only a couple of matches, one of which was against Sussex at Guildford. It was what might be termed an old-fashioned county pitch, grassy but not firm, really a club wicket, with each ball taking out little divots. There were a few current England batsmen appearing, like Kenny Barrington, Jim Parks and myself, and we all struggled for runs. For Peter it was not a problem. Once again, he used the airborne route for the ball which was pitched up. He had no inhibitions about hitting it over the top and made it very difficult for the bowlers to find any sort of length. He was head and shoulders above the rest of us.

The trademark shot of Peter May was the on-drive, which he could place either side of mid-on with equal

PETER MAY: *He might have appeared to be the personification of the English gentleman, but that character became superseded by tigerish qualities when he took the field.*

facility. He had a slightly strong right-hand grip, but his head was always right over the ball that was slightly overpitched on middle-and-leg. Despite this strong right-hand grip, his cover play, both along the ground and in the air, was extremely powerful. Everything was set up for him to hit the ball to leg, so how was he so strong in the cover area as well?

The fact was that, when he saw the opportunity to play through the off side, he would turn the whole of his upper body so that, from the other end, you saw him virtually turn his back on the ball. Never mind just turning the left shoulder into the shot, he really turned round slightly to flat-bat it through and over the off side. By turning so far round, it was almost as if he was still playing it to leg, whereas in reality the ball went speeding through the covers.

Peter May was the quiet, introspective man off the field who turned into an aggressive predator on it. It was a trait reflected in his captaincy as well. He might have appeared to be the personification of the English gentleman, but that character became superseded by tigerish qualities when he took the field at the head of a team and there was a match to be won. Obviously a complex individual, Peter May remained an enigma with two diametrically opposed perceptions of his character.

The Flight of the Dodo

Leg-spin was always a bit of an Achilles Heel for Dexter, the batsman. As someone who, with all due modesty, had a more than reasonable record as a batsman, I did manage to get out to leg-spinners on a significant number of occasions. On my first tour as captain of England, I had a successful time in India and Pakistan in 1961–62. That was until I came to the fourth and fifth Tests and fell under the spell of Chandra Borde. I had scored 57 in Calcutta when I was yorked playing over the top of a loopy, full-length ball. In Madras I did exactly the same thing, except that I had only made 2 at the time. When I got back to the dressing-room, Kenny Barrington chirped up with a statement of the blindingly obvious, 'Seems like he's found your weakness, Captain,' as I kicked the table over in a rare display of frustration.

There were others, too. When playing against Bobby Simpson of Australia, I was determined to learn to sweep. It had never been my strong point, yet I saw everybody else collecting the ball off leg-stump. It was an annoyance to me that I could not perfect the shot. I was always looking to cut or drive, and you do not really want to be driving leg-spinners unless you can help it. It is much better to hit the short ball, but the sweep is useful when they drift down the leg-stump and you have virtually a free hit.

One of my early meetings with the Australian tourists in 1961 was at Lord's when I was playing for MCC.

I regarded this as the perfect opportunity to learn to sweep. It was one up to Simpson! He went two up in the second innings of the first Test. I was batting to save what turned out to be a drawn game with 180 to my name. There were only about two overs remaining when Simpson came on for a final spell. I had visions of a double-century, waltzed down the wicket, missed it and was stumped by Wally Grout.

It was later on that same tour that England suffered that famous collapse at Old Trafford when, in a somewhat desperate move, Richie Benaud resorted to bowling round the wicket. England, set 256 runs to win in 230 minutes, were well on target. I must admit that I began the rot by trying to cut a ball that went across me and bounced a bit. Wally Grout was again the man who completed the dismissal and we were on our way to defeat. From 150 for 1 at one stage we were all out for 201.

I did gain a certain amount of revenge against Richie on the 1962–63 tour. I managed to get after him and do a bit of damage to his figures, but even then he accounted for me six times in ten Test innings. Earlier, in India, there was another leg-spinner, Subhash Gupte, who was posing a bit of a threat. He bowled us out cheaply in the first innings at Kanpur by taking five wickets, E. R. Dexter among them. I had heard that he tended to wilt a bit if someone got after him, so when we followed-on I attacked him and I got a nice, big hundred. He pretty well retired hurt from that encounter, being dropped after the next Test.

RICHIE BENAUD: I managed to get after him and do a bit of damage to his figures, but even then he accounted for me six times in ten Test innings.

They did not have to be leg-spinners of renown to claim my wicket. In Johannesburg in 1964–65, I was well past my hundred overnight on the most perfect of batting wickets and the quickest outfield on which I had ever played. It was a wonderful opportunity to bat and, as I moved into the 170s, I was seriously contemplating the world record. That was when the captain introduced a new bowler into the attack. Graeme Pollock had only bowled thirteen overs in Test cricket before that, and had not taken a single wicket at that level. He was the most occasional leg-spinner to be found, yet he had me caught at the wicket in his first over.

Despite their successes against me, it was not long before the leg-spinner went into a decline so marked that the breed was virtually extinct in first-class cricket. Suddenly, there has been a major resurgence in the art, and the game as a whole is all the better for it. It is not just at the top level, either. Look at any playground where games of pick-up cricket are being played or go to any coaching session for youngsters. You will see a host of would-be leg-spinners wheeling away, giving the ball a tweak out of the back of the hand. Leg-spin has returned in a big way.

You have to look back to Abdul Qadir of Pakistan to find the seeds of this remarkable transformation. He was pretty much alone as a leg-spinner in the very top flight for quite a while. He had a very individual style, being a very aggressive cricketer with a violent action and a wide variety of deliveries, to say nothing of a tremendous line in appealing. But it is true to say that, even with Qadir's success, there was not a long queue of others of his type trying to break into cricket at the top level.

There were signs of leg-spin re-emerging when India came to England in 1990. In the one-day internationals they not only played a leg-spinner, but beat England out of sight in the two matches. Anil Kumble won the man-of-the-match award in the first of those matches with figures of 2 for 29 from 11 high-quality overs. At the time, I have to say, I wondered whether they had not really discovered something about one-day cricket. The World Cup was not that far away and the thought crossed my mind that, if they can beat England as easily as that using a certain amount of leg-spin to dampen a powerful England batting line-up, I genuinely fancied them to win the competition. The other Indian leg-spinner in that touring party was Narendra Hirwani, and he finished top of the tour bowling averages, just in front of Kumble. This suggested that leg-spin might be on the way back.

Then Shane Warne burst on to the scene, and now any self-respecting Test side feels ill-equipped if there is not a wrist spinner either in or on the verge of the team. It is a delightful coincidence that I am writing this piece on 13 November 1995. I have just heard on the radio that Warne has taken eleven wickets in the match as Australia beat Pakistan by an innings. His first innings exploits are detailed in the *Daily Telegraph* this morning while, across the page, I can read about Hirwani taking 6 wickets for India against New Zealand, and that Kumble is in the team as well. The photograph in the centre of the page is of Devon Malcolm shaking the hand of Paul Adams, the left-arm wrist spinner with the extraordinary action, bowling South Africa 'A' to victory over the England tourists. You can only assume that not only is leg-spin back but proving to be extremely effective at the highest level.

You have to ask the question whether their success is due to the fact that batsmen have not had the practice and so do not know how to combat this type of bowling? Whatever the situation, it is a wonderful development for cricket. The game will only thrive on variety and the leg-spinner certainly brings that to the game. However, one needs to look a little closer at the success of Shane Warne as the first really young, strong leg-spinner to have such a devastating effect. Any team would appreciate the benefit of having him in their side, whoever it is and whoever they were playing against.

Shane Warne became so good so quickly while practising an art which, in the Richie Benaud era, was always accepted would take a long time to mature. My thought about Shane Warne is that, because of his great power of spin, it is quite natural for the ball to drift in through the air towards the leg side. With the ball pitching leg-stump or just outside, which might be thought of as a negative line to bowl in conventional terms, he naturally does not go for many runs. Traditionally the leg-spinner would be put on against the quality batsmen and, if the bowler was not successful straight away, the batsman would pick him off at five or six runs an over. The captain looked at the scoreboard which had advanced rapidly by some thirty runs. He felt he had lost control, the batsmen were getting set and enjoying themselves, so the captain would take the bowler off. Warne tends to go for only two runs an over, the captain is happy, and so he is left on to bowl nice long spells. That allows him to warm to his task, his confidence grows and he learns to bowl. One thing

SHANE WARNE: A blond-haired archetypal Australian lad with a huge profile.

leads to another and thus a top-class bowler emerges at an unprecedented early age.

Anil Kumble was doing much the same but kept the runs down in a slightly different way. A tall man with a very high action, a lot of energy, and most of the balls running on and dipping in, he bowls a good line and seldom tries to turn the ball away from the bat. In fact, in his homeland he is known as a top-spinner rather than a leg-spinner. He might say he does not bowl them, but it looks to me as if he bowls quite a lot of flippers. Again, he got to bowl plenty of overs and so learned his trade.

Narendra Hirwani had not enjoyed the same learning period when he made an extraordinary Test début. He took sixteen wickets on that occasion against the West Indies in Madras in 1988. That could be put down to novelty value and a West Indian batting side totally flummoxed by this style of attack. After touring England in 1990, he rather fell away and was hardly seen again until re-emerging in 1995 to help India win the series against New Zealand.

The great news is that in Australia, and elsewhere, youngsters are queuing up to bowl wrist-spin. Shane Warne is this blond-haired archetypal Australian lad with a huge profile and proving to be extremely successful. When you ally those qualities to the fact that he is becoming very wealthy from cricket, it is not surprising that the youngsters want to copy him. They would now rather bowl leg-spin like Shane than go down to the beach. It is wonderful to think that cricket has become more glamorous than surfing.

In the Swing

I have witnessed two outstanding pieces of swing bowling in all my time of playing or watching Test cricket. Coincidentally, both occurred at Lord's. The ball does not always swing on this ground, but there is no doubt that it did swing in spectacular fashion for the Pakistani bowlers in 1992, as it had for the Australian Bob Massie exactly twenty years before. What made 'Massie's Match' so remarkable was the fact that the Western Australian was making his début in Test cricket, and had not enjoyed the best of fortune on the earlier part of the tour. A return of 6 for 31 at Worcester in the opening match promised much, but at Lord's in the MCC match he had broken down with a side strain after bowling just nine balls. There was no evidence to suggest that he would make such a dramatic entry to the Test arena.

In 1972 I was writing for the *Sunday Mirror* and saw all of this remarkable Test. It is true to say that conditions were absolutely perfect for conventional, 'shiny' swing but, even so, the movement that Bob Massie achieved was prodigious. I had never seen anything like it. Batsmen could hardly lay a bat on the ball, while the bowler had to ensure that it was sufficiently on line to get wickets. To the left-handers, Massie went around the wicket and still swung it both ways with devastating effect. However, the in-swinger, coming down from round the wicket, was colossal.

Conditions were right, and the bowler was just the right pace to exploit them to the full. Much quicker and he might not have got such alarming movement; much slower and it would not have been as effective.

Having said that, Dennis Lillee got the ball to swing more in that game than I had seen him manage before or since. My suspicions were aroused, enabling me to get what might be termed the one scoop of my newspaper career. I telephoned Tony Greig to ask him exactly what was happening out in the middle. He said it was a routine occurrence – they were using lip ice, and had done so also at Old Trafford in the first Test. I had never even heard of lip ice, let alone how it could be used to the bowler's advantage. He explained that it was the clear stuff applied to the lips to stop them burning in hot climates. Now it was being used to polish the ball. I asked if I could quote him. He refused that, but assured me it was happening.

I went down to the chemist and asked for a sample of every brand of lip ice they had in stock. I received some quizzical looks, but got them, went home, got out an old ball and a rag impregnated with lip ice, and started to polish. I got the shock of my life. The ball came up like a mirror. I rang my editor, Tony Smith, and told him that I had something he ought to see. I had roughened up the ball once more, gave him the rag and told him to have a go. Again, it shone like a new ball, and I told him that the Australians were using the same trick in matches.

In those days I still felt a little sensitive to the fact that I was a fairly recently retired ex-cricketer and felt that it might be letting the side down to expose a matter like this. I went to see the Australian manager, Bob Steele, to warn him that we had rumbled his bowlers and would be running the story in a big way. It was a fairly terse interview in which he was totally non-committal. There was no doubt, however, that from then on the ball stopped swinging in the way it had at Lord's. I am sure that action was taken by the manager, who might not have even known himself what had been going on before I told him. Bob Massie took four more wickets in the first innings of the next Test at Trent Bridge, but then bowled another 109 overs in the series, taking a mere three more wickets.

Twenty years later at Lord's, history was repeated. In 1992 it was the Pakistani pace attack of Wasim Akram and Waqar Younis who were swinging the ball all over the place, and doing so at a phenomenal pace. Wasim had missed the first Test, which was a high-scoring draw, but he was back to partner Waqar at Lord's as the pair ripped the heart out of England. Wasim, in particular, was quite devastating with the old ball, because this was an example of reverse swing as opposed to shiny swing.

What really stands out in my memory are two consecutive deliveries to Jack Russell. Wasim was bowling left-arm round-the-wicket to the left-hander, and the first one pitched well outside leg-stump on a full length. The batsman shaped to turn it round the corner. It swung away so sharply that it just missed the off-stump. It fizzed through to the 'keeper with the batsman totally opened up. The next ball, still from round the wicket, set off in

*WAQAR YOUNIS AND WASIM AKRAM: At Lord's in 1992
they were swinging the ball all over the place, and doing so at a
phenomenal pace.*

the general direction of first slip before coming back the
other way to uproot middle-stump.

During that series, both Waqar and Wasim produced
an extent of swing and a lateness of swing with the old
ball that I had never witnessed before. You can judge
what it was like because, only the previous summer, the

English batsmen had managed to hang around for a long time against the pace of the West Indies. Derek Pringle had managed to play some lengthy innings, young Mark Ramprakash had come into the side and hung around for a long time, and even lower-order batsmen like Phillip DeFreitas, Chris Lewis and Richard Illingworth had their moments. Now, twelve months later, they could not even lay a bat on the ball.

It was total devastation, and I am not even sure that the high-order batsmen would have been much better off against the old ball. Reverse swing being what it is, the early batsmen had fifty or sixty overs before the ball really started behaving strangely, and Waqar in particular hardly got the new ball to swing at all. For reverse swing to be effective, one side needs to be as wet as possible. This makes one side of the old ball relatively smooth, if not shiny. It is a debatable point whether wetting the ball with saliva, perspiration, or anything else, is permitted. People might say that if you can use spit to shine it, why not use spit to wet it? It is a grey area.

While one side is made wet, it is absolutely essential to keep the other side totally dry. Hence, perhaps, the Atherton incident when I believe he was just trying to make sure his fingers were dry so that when he touched the ball he did not put any sweat on the dry side. This dry side should, ideally, be worn so that the surface is actually rough, and the suggestion is that, if it is rough near the seam, it has a good aerodynamic effect. My feeling is that in the early days, when reverse swing was first discovered, bowlers tended to have a little pick with their nails to rough it up. However, as time went on, it was found that might not be necessary. Then the umpires began looking at the ball and it happened even less.

History repeated itself when batsmen started to draw attention to the state of the ball. Just as I had been tipped off about the use of lip ice in 1972, so Allan Lamb made public his concerns over unnatural wear on the ball in 1992. It is my belief that, if it is possible to get the ball into a condition to favour reverse swing naturally, it does take a little longer than if the process is speeded up by an outside agency.

So how do the likes of Waqar Younis achieve reverse swing? For the right-arm bowler, the very successful ball has been the late in-swinger. It is bowled with the smooth side on the right as it goes down the pitch. This is in the same position as for the out-swinger, with an identical grip and an identical action. The difference is that, instead of leaving the right-handed batsman, it will dip in late. Imran Khan was one of the first to master it, but Waqar has so perfected it that his feared 'toe crusher' has taken its toll of many a batsman.

When considering conventional swing, we have to think back to the time when whoever took the new ball was expected to swing it. It is possible that some critical stage in the manufacture of a cricket ball changed, because quite suddenly that swing disappeared. Of course, it could be that all the correct actions disappeared at the same time. It is hard to know, although there has been the odd conventional swinger of the ball who has the sort of action which has always made swing more likely.

Pace and length also come into the equation. There is no doubt that there were natural swing bowlers who lost the knack as a result of the type of cricket which was played. Chris Lewis and Phillip DeFreitas are two cases in point. As youngsters they were both consistent away-swingers of the ball, yet in mid-career with England they could scarcely swing one if they tried. They put their fingers on top of the ball, banging it down into the pitch and angled in at the batsman. If the ball hits the pitch halfway down, it has not had a chance to swing.

That is very much a product of one-day cricket where a delivery angled in at the batsman is the percentage delivery. The ball leaving the bat in one-day cricket can be edged through the vacant slip area and produces runs; the ball taking the inside edge crashes into the pads and goes for a scampered single at worst. Bowlers are not so versatile that they can turn it on and off as required. Looking back, Fred Trueman could be guaranteed to come on with the new ball, pitch it up and swing it. It presented a major problem to Australians who liked to go back and nudge to the leg side. Norman O'Neill, for example, was a candidate every time he was in at the right time. We'd give Fred the new ball and Colin Cowdrey would routinely pick him up at slip.

If conventional swing has declined, reverse swing has become an innovation which has almost taken its place. There is no doubt that this technique has been a major development in the game with as much impact in modern times as the introduction of the googly at the turn of the century. Now that umpires have become aware of the implications of ball tampering, reverse swing should only occur through natural processes. There was a story that Ken Palmer got thoroughly fed up with the behaviour on the field in 1992, involving total lack of respect for the umpires. When he examined the ball he suspected that there might have been some unnatural wear and tear, but there was no real evidence for making an issue of it.

At one point, so the story goes, he lost his cool and decided to deal with matters on his own. He made sure that his hand was really wet when the ball was thrown to him for an inspection, and promptly splashed the dry side into his wet palm. Once it was thoroughly soaked, he threw it back to the bowler and looked on, amused at the consternation and uproar which ensued. That incident went unpublicised, but in February 1995 Salim Malik and Aamir Sohail of Pakistan effected an interesting variation on the theme when they reported the Zimbabwean umpire, Ian Robinson, to the match referee for wetting one side of the ball during a Test in Harare. A case of reverse tampering?

The Charm and Genius of 'Compo'

It was a source of immense pleasure for me that I managed to take the field a few times with Denis Compton. I came on to the scene right at the end of his career, playing against him in the Gentlemen v. Players fixture at Lord's. Even in this brief acquaintance I found the old stories about him to be true. It was already a legend in the game that he would turn up for the first match of the season without any practice, pick up the first bat which came to hand and go out to score an exhilarating hundred. Similarly, he would arrive late for a big match, find his side was batting, and so have a sleep in the dressing-room, then be woken up and go out to play an innings only a genius could play. And all the time he could charm the birds out of the trees.

Even though he was in the twilight of his career, he could still show what a genius he was with a bat in his hand. We played some Cavaliers cricket together, and on this particular occasion we were playing on a rain-affected club pitch in Surrey. Most of our side were current Test players, with a batting order which would have done credit to a World XI. On the other side there was a young quick bowler by the name of Alan Ward, just making a name for himself, and keen to enhance it by knocking over a few of the stars of view.

Alan Ward was to become a genuinely quick bowler for Derbyshire and England for the short time that injury allowed this spindly 6′ 3″-tall bowler to function at full bore. As a youngster on this Sunday afternoon in Surrey, he was out to prove himself on a pitch where every ball took chunks out. It was a real flyer. Batsmen like Barrington, Sobers, Kanhai and Dexter had been skittled out by Ward. Compo went in at number six, the ball was still misbehaving, and he got a fifty without any problem. Whatever was bowled at him found the middle of his bat.

When he eventually came off I remarked what a fantastic performance it had been. He made an observation to the effect that, when the ball is lifting, there is no point in getting too close to it. Of course, he was absolutely right. Get in behind the lifting ball and all that is likely to happen is that it will hit you on the gloves and you will offer a catch. He said that if it is lifting, as it was, you had to stand away from it. The ball can sail by, if it is dropped short you can cut it or, if it is overpitched, you can still get forward and drive. We had all been trying to bat in the normal way by getting in behind it, and getting out. He said that was the last thing we should have been trying to do. It was evidence of his genius. For him it came naturally, which was why he could make it look so simple.

I still have a clip of cine film of him making his last hundred. He was playing for the International Cavaliers at Sabina Park, Jamaica, in 1963–64. The opposition did not want him to fail, so they gave him his first ten. From then on they tried all they knew, yet he never looked like getting out. He was forty-five at the time, but it was still a most attractive innings, the ball still hit the middle of the bat without fail, and the celebrated sweep was still there.

The amazing thing about the Compton sweep was the backlift. Nowadays, batsmen tend to pick the bat up early. The point about Denis's sweep was that he had the bat down and never picked it up if he was going to play the shot. When he saw the ball to sweep, he pushed the bat forward and popped the ball on its way. It was what came naturally to him, yet for other shots, he would pick the bat up in a conventional manner. He was a good hooker and cutter, both shots demanding a high backlift, and he would pick it up too when he was going to drive. What he would not do is pick it up too early. It was still down and waiting, but once he saw the ball coming a little down the leg side, the bat would go forward and straight into the sweep.

Perhaps the greatest demonstration of his genius came even later. He must have been well over fifty when he played in an inter-newspaper game between the *Sunday Express* and the *Sunday Mirror*. Denis had gout, was nominally captain of the side, but did not field. He stayed in the bar, having a few drinks while being as charming and genial to everyone as ever. However, the game became a little tight. Suddenly the *Express* were nine wickets down in the last over needing 6 to win. It seemed like at least ten minutes went by as Compton struggled into a pair of whites, strapped on some pads, picked up a bat and ambled to the middle.

By now it was getting very gloomy and there was a big,

DENIS COMPTON: A batsman of sheer genius.

keen lad waiting at the end of his run to rush up and bowl at him. Compo had all the old mannerisms. There was a twiddle of the bat and a look round the field, he had a laugh with the wicket-keeper, and settled down to face the ball that the bowler intended should be the last of the match. It was. Despite the fact that he had not held a bat for some years, the light was bad and the bowler was no slouch, Denis Compton took a couple of steps towards him as he was about to deliver. Seeing this, the bowler banged the ball in the middle of the pitch. 'Compo' took a little short-arm bang at it and hit it right out of the ground.

A big grin spread across his face as he looked round and said, 'Thanks, boys; nice game'. As he ambled off in the direction from which he had come just a few moments before, I could scarcely believe what I had seen. It was not as if it was a wild swing at the ball. He kept a steady head, looked at it, and dispatched it right off of the middle of the bat, as usual. Only a batsman of sheer genius could contemplate the shot; only a man of supreme charm could accomplish it without a trace of arrogance.

The Classical School of English Batting

In recent times there have been a couple of key changes in the English approach to batting. It might be envy or sour grapes on my part, but as I finished my playing career I noticed a sickening fall in the quality of English batting. There was also a change in selection personnel with the likes of Alec Bedser and Doug Insole taking over from the Gubby Allen and R. W. V. Robins era. Different personalities, taking selection into what might be termed a professional era.

The type of batsman available for selection had, it is true, changed. May had retired early because of illness; Dexter had gone because he had other fish to fry and had a broken leg. I remember being really quite shocked that, when the new batting selections came along, they included, for instance, Tom Graveney, who was even older than I was, and John Edrich, already in his thirties and not good enough to play before some of the others had gone. It seemed that we had missed a beat. They both happened to do very well, so they could be regarded as good selections, but I just wonder if there had not been a break in the thread which had come down from Hutton, May, Cowdrey, Dexter and the like.

That might or might not have been a pivotal point in the development of batting in this country. What is certain is that another crucial moment occurred when Kerry Packer and his World Series Cricket arrived on the scene in 1977. Virtually the whole of the England First XI were taken away and we were left with Geoff Boycott, who might not have been the best player at passing on knowledge to others, and Mike Brearley who would only just pass muster as a Test player. I felt very strongly at that time that there was going to be a break in the line of communication down through the ages. I am sure that we had all learned about Test cricket from those we batted with when we first got in the side. I know how I had learned from Peter May, for he had a way of communicating what was needed if players were going to succeed at Test level.

I even went as far as trying to find commercial backing to run top quality coaching for the next generation of aspiring Test players in order to try to bridge that gap. I was going to get the best coaches and the best former Test players such as the Cowdreys and Mays to come and get hold of these young guys. For one reason or another it never happened, but I think that break in the thread did become apparent when there was nobody to help them find their way and they had to learn from scratch.

You could say that it was a refreshing release, so that someone like Gower could just come in and play like Gower, but perhaps Gower might have been an even better player with some extra help and guidance. Gubby Allen once said in David Gower's early days, 'If only he could be persuaded to move his foot just six inches in the back stroke, I don't think they would get him out from one year to the next.' Just occasionally his footwork was a little bit static. Had there been someone of stature at the other end at an impressionable stage of Gower's career, he might have learned and benefited from the help without it in any way stifling his undoubted natural flair. That talent might have been harnessed to better effect for the team and the player.

Then there was the situation where six batsmen would be going out to bat for England who were not only all totally different in the way they went about the task, but all totally unorthodox. At one period Tony Greig and Alan Knott were actually getting nearly all of England's runs. Tony was a terrific competitor, very brave and very aggressive, but there was little real quality about his batting. He just went for it as he saw fit. Alan Knott was even more weird. He was very talented, but just worked it out from day to day and came up with all sorts of funny theories about where he put his left hand, how to get the bat high to fend off the fast bowlers and where the head should be. I have had lots of arguments with Alan over the years about such matters.

The orthodox stream of batting had been interrupted; then you had Mike Brearley as the first person to come out with a helmet and an early lift of the bat. Someone had told him he was falling over too much to the off side and if he kept his head up that would not happen. He believed if he had to get his head up, he should get the bat up as well and suddenly we had the early backlift brigade and I wonder whether it will ever settle down again. We have Robin Smith with a successful career, but it terrifies me when I see him in slow motion. The bat starts lifted and he virtually plays two strokes to every ball. How he has the time to do it I shall never know. The bat is lifted, then it comes down to a mid-point as the ball is on its way before going up again and coming down all round the houses. It looks doubtful if he could ever get a ball in the middle of the bat. And he is reckoned to be one of the straighter England players!

When, as Chairman of Selectors, I took over the England side in 1989, we really did have a liquorice allsorts of a batting line-up. Kim Barnett played, dancing around and waving his bat about the place. Peter Willey got squarer and squarer. The demise of proper footwork can be traced back to Dennis Amiss, for he was just a solid front-foot and straight-bat player. He was very good at it, but his footwork was poor and his cross-bat play was poor. His right elbow flew right up in the air so he could not physically get the toe of the bat up and get into position to play with a cross-bat. It was fine to play straight, but he missed out on so many scoring opportunities from cross-batted shots. Furthermore, Lillee sorted him out for a pastime as he was never in the right place to handle it.

Mike Gatting should have been a nice, orthodox player, but his footwork was ghastly. For all it mattered, he could have had a six-inch nail through his right foot because it never did, and still does not, move anywhere. It made him a wonderful striker in limited-overs cricket where the ball gets pitched up and, because he is enormously skilled, whenever he is attacking the bowler he gets results. However, in a Test Match when he was not in a position to attack he was always vulnerable, as seen by the length of time it took him to establish himself in Test cricket. Then he had a reasonably successful period, before it all fell away again. He was fallible all his Test career.

Chris Broad's bat was never ever straight. He had a weird pick-up, playing inside to out on the off side and outside to in on the leg side. He was big, determined, skilled, professional and a good guy. When you have all those qualities and are playing almost every day, you should be able to make almost anything work – up to a standard. Not, though, up to a quality standard.

Graham Gooch is another. He has been enormously successful, but when you look back at film of the early Gooch, with his bat on the ground, he actually looks twice the player. If he could have stayed that way and gained the experience, he might have been more successful earlier. Kenny Barrington was yet another. Here was an orthodox, quality player who graduated to the Test arena, lost his place and then completely modified his batting. Again, it was very successful but with limitations. If he had stayed where he was and gained the vital experience to make his original quality play work, I think he would have been better served.

It became particularly evident where English batting had gone wrong when we played Sri Lanka in a one-off Test at Lord's in 1984. A succession of Sri Lankan batsmen came in, each one of them with the bat on the ground, each one moved his feet, everyone was beautifully straight, and everyone could pull and hook.

The general impression was that they were much better players than our guys. The fact that they could score 491 for 7 declared in their first innings at Lord's illustrated that the Sri Lankans had inherited what should have been English qualities. Certainly the public noticed the difference between the two sides and their approach to batting. There were so many comments about the textbook style exhibited by the visitors that you would have thought correct batting was an innovation. It just went to show that we had completely lost our way.

It needs someone like Michael Atherton to show up the others. His success makes you think that perhaps there was not so much wrong with the orthodox in the first place. Here is a man who is not brimming over with talent for hitting a cricket ball. He is not short of talent, but would not be rated in the genius area. He times his cover-drive and his cut well enough, but he misses a few as well and it is his orthodoxy which pulls him through, along with his guts and his brains. Graeme Hick is not unorthodox, and is developing as he goes along. Graham Thorpe is a punchy left-hander and is not far away from an acceptable standard, so perhaps we are getting back a little orthodoxy. We need to, for our batting was pretty weird for far too long. It is extraordinary that England, the one full-time professional outfit in world cricket, should have bred so many oddities and misfits.

'Middle and Head, Please, Umpire'

Newcomers to the game wonder about this strange, sacred rite that batsmen go through when they get to the crease, namely taking guard. When you think that they either take leg, middle-and-leg, or middle, you might ask whether placing the bat two and a half inches one way or the other really matters, particularly as the batsman's head position can vary by anything up to a foot. So what is the batsman trying to achieve when he takes guard, and what guard should he take?

Certainly against quick bowlers from the Pavilion End at Lord's I used to take my normal middle-and-leg guard, but then go over another two inches or so towards the off side to cover the movement of the ball down the slope. That means that I was actually taking off-stump guard, but I never wanted to ask the umpire for off-stump because I thought he would then consider me a prime candidate for LBW.

Against quick bowling in general I tended to move across towards off-stump as it is necessary to pre-select to an extent because there is not time to make big movements. Since you want to be over in the area on or just outside off-stump, you might as well be there in the first place. The only point in standing away to leg is to make room to hit the ball on the off side when it happens to be overpitched. Against very fast bowlers, especially when you first go in, you are not looking to hit booming drives, so you might as well be over there ready, knowing where the off-stump is, and knowing that anything wide can safely be left alone.

All the batsman is trying to do when he takes guard is position his feet to enable his head to be in line with the middle stump. In that way he knows where his wicket is and the line of the ball in relation to it. Some batsmen show a lot of wicket because they stand away from their bats, while others offer the bowler only a glimpse of the stumps because they stand right in to their bats. That is unimportant. What counts is the position of the head.

I recently heard that the Olympic gold medallist Jim Fox trained pistol shooters in the Modern Pentathlon by getting them to stand in position, close their eyes and raise the pistol towards the target. On opening their eyes, the marksmen had to judge where they were aiming. If it was to the left of centre, they had to shuffle their feet round to the right, or vice-versa, so that their natural stance allowed them to be aiming at the bull without making any compensatory body movements when actually firing the gun. Perhaps batsmen should go to the crease, take up their normal stance, and ask the umpire to tell them when their head is in line with middle stump?

On the Run

What a mess some bowlers manage to make of what should be the simple part of the job. Getting from their bowling mark to the point of delivery should present few problems, yet what I see pains me. I see extraordinary hops, skips and jumps in run-ups, leading me to wonder whoever helped the young bowler in his formative years. What a pity they did not get them merely to run up to the wicket and bowl.

Instead you can find bowlers apparently trying to gather themselves to bowl in every stride. To take the faster bowlers, all they should be doing is running towards the delivery point while establishing rhythm and building up momentum to get up to a certain speed. The speed of the bowler on reaching the crease does actually provide a percentage of the pace of the ball. In some bowlers it is more than others, but it is somewhere between five and getting on for twenty per cent of the pace of the ball. There is, therefore, something to be said for being fast through the crease, but not to the extent of losing balance and being unable to use all the attributes of a good action.

The mere fact of marking out the run can be a study in itself at times. I was once watching Devon Malcolm go through the process. He started out at the crease and worked it out backwards. In principle, that is a good way of doing it. I have always felt that I can decide where I want my left foot to land, run away from the stumps, and where I land my left foot at the other end is the point of departure. There are problems associated with this method if there is a pronounced slope or strong wind of which to take account. Of course, you have that problem whichever method you use.

There are simple ways of measuring a run, but people still have difficulty in achieving it. I have never understood why they do not use a length of twine. They could go out before the start, measure their run by using the twine and put their mark down. I have never seen anyone do that, but I am reminded that Simon Hughes, of Middlesex and then Durham, twigged the problem. He measured his run accurately by going out before the start of play and measuring exact boot lengths – heel to toe, heel to toe – and found that with this precise run he bowled very few no-balls.

I had a little bit to do with Simon Hughes's development. He is an Ealing boy, living close by, and his father asked me to have a look at him when he was a lad. He was supposed to be an all-rounder, but when I saw him batting I discovered an awful lot of funny things going on. His bowling, however, looked terrific. He was athletic, had a good action, and was one of those who could be safely told to continue with what he was doing.

That was off just a few paces in the indoor school. I did not see him bowl properly for three or four years, by which time he was getting into the Middlesex side. Then I was horrified to discover that he had an absolute mess of a run-up. Every approach was different, with

BOB WILLIS: With legs churning and arms pumping to get the momentum he needed to bowl.

changing elements coming into play, and his bowling reflected the lack of consistency in the run. I was moved to have a word with him, pointing out his woeful run-up. He resisted doing anything about it for about two more years before he eventually began to get himself a bit more organised. He saw me one day and admitted that he must have been pretty thick not to listen to me in the first place.

Bob Willis came to Australia in 1970–71 as a late replacement to join Ray Illingworth's team. Perhaps it was the strange conditions for him, with harder pitches than he had ever encountered before, but his run-up went completely awry. I cannot claim to have been particularly successful, but I did tell him about what I regard as a really useful device when bowlers are struggling to find any sort of rhythm in their run.

I get them right away from any pitch or pitch markings. Then I put down a cap or whatever and tell them to run from there across the outfield until they feel they are ready to bowl. To start with, I do not even put down a mark where they do actually bowl from. I just get them used to running and bowling without any restrictions or inhibitions. By keeping an eye on where they reach before they bowl, it is possible to discern a pattern and find a natural run for the bowler. He is just aware of his body and his rhythm and the rest develops on its own. Bob Willis did start to find this exercise helpful. He changed it again later on, but became a pretty good runner-in, with legs churning and arms pumping to get the momentum he needed to bowl.

To achieve rhythm, I found it useful to think in groups of four paces. Start off with, say, the left foot and go left, right, left, right, as a little starter. Then put in another group of four, then another, until you know you have reached full momentum, and then bowl. It takes you through all the stages of the run. Remember, you will be starting in virtually a stationary position and the first group of four gets you going, you gather momentum towards a peak and then, moving as fast as necessary while maintaining balance, you bowl.

Another practice which strikes me as wrong-headed is to put down your mark and then go back another ten yards or so past it before starting the run. The bowler who does this invariably stutters up to the mark before finally getting off on the correct foot. A check mark as well as a starting mark can be a useful device, but I doubt if many bowlers need one if they start correctly in the first place.

I have always thought that, by and large, slow bowlers should run up like any other bowler, but with a shorter approach. They do not need the momentum, but balance becomes absolutely vital. They have no margin for error, but there is every reason why they should be able to maintain balance and consistency. Having said that, there have been a number of exceptions to the rule. Derek Underwood had a good, smooth run-up, as did Richie Benaud. Jim Laker, on the other hand, did not really run up, and nor does Shane Warne.

In my time, the master of a smooth run-up was Brian Statham. All the time I was his captain, standing at mid-off, he would just have a little word on the way back if things were not exactly right. 'I haven't quite got the rhythm today, Captain,' was all he would say, because rhythm was the vital ingredient of his bowling. He was a perfect example of trying to find rhythm and relaxation, and without the latter he could not find the

BRIAN STATHAM: The master of the smooth run-up.

former.

He knew that he could not start to bowl the ball until he actually got to the crease. So many bowlers begin to tense up as they go down the run. The good ones are still relaxed some four or five strides out. Men like Richard Hadlee were relaxed right up to the delivery, and so was John Snow who was a wonderful runner as well. Fred Trueman might vary a bit. Sometimes he could be spot-on and be scampering in while at other times he might struggle for his stride. On this subject you have to mention Michael Holding, whose run simply oozed feline grace. There again, he was a superb athlete with a quarter-miler's efficiency of movement.

Holding is an example of how a good bowler so often has a good run-up. There are exceptions to this rule as well. The Australian Neil Hawke had no more than an ungainly shuffle into the wicket and then a massive shoulder heave. He did, however, manage to use that approach and action to get considerable movement, and had a well-disguised slower ball. Then there are those who run for miles and miles, and how they ever arrive at the same point two balls in succession, I cannot imagine. Hampshire and England had a big, burly quick bowler by the name of David 'Butch' White, and I once tried to run-up in his footsteps. I got hopelessly lost somewhere along the forty-five yard arc that brought him to the crease.

On the subject of speed through the crease, bowlers like Malcolm Marshall and Mike Procter both used to generate their pace from the arm rather than a body action, so the quicker the body was moving over the crease the better it was for them. On the whole I believe it is better to be faster rather than slower through the creases, even if some people tend to overdo the rush in to bowl. If they are all momentum and no balance, they are unlikely to do themselves justice. Just as with

MICHAEL HOLDING: *His run simply oozed feline grace.*

so many aspects of the game, there is a need to maintain an equilibrium: momentum up to the crease and balance through it.

Field Sports

What a drag fielding can be; but the day when you start looking up at the clock and wondering how long it is to the next interval is the day when you should seriously consider getting out of the game. It means that you have to take a positive attitude, be enthusiastic and develop your skills. Above all, you have to allow yourself to enjoy it and feel part of the team. You have to be on the side of the bowler, prepared to bust a gut to help him, whether it is concentrating for slip catches or saving those extra few runs in the field.

I was an enthusiast, if nothing else, in my early days. I might have been a bit wild at times, but it was born of wanting to be better at this part of the game. At the very start of my career, Cyril Washbrook of Lancashire and England was noted for being a fine fielder, and he seemed to be a good model to try to emulate. He was to be found in the covers, was fast over the ground and had a very accurate throw. He also had a little trick whereby he would always throw back to the 'keeper. He would not hold it and pass it on to the bowler, but made a point of banging it in to the 'keeper, hard over the top. He would do that for a few overs and then he might spot the non-striker just a little tardy when it came to making his ground. Still looking at the wicket-keeper, he could throw the ball sideways at the stumps at the bowler's end and picked up quite a few victims that way.

Cyril was an example of somebody developing fielding

to reach a new level, and that does not happen often. Some of the Australians managed to do so in my time having come from a baseball background. Neil Harvey was a case in point. A good mover and well balanced, he had a fine arm for a small man and had developed it from baseball. Anybody who plays baseball as a youngster learns how to throw. That does not necessarily happen with cricket. Cricket books tend to be uninformative on the subject, just passing over it. There are only three ways of returning the ball. There is the little underarm throw which saves time if you are close to the stumps. In certain cases, if you are running to the side and have to get the ball in quickly, there is a side-arm throw, although it is not the most accurate. The rest of the time, the throw has to be straight over the top of the shoulder.

In one season of play I twice saw Mark Ramprakash pick the ball up and send in a side-arm throw, and twice I saw the ball finish up some five yards from the stumps on the half-volley. England's throwing is generally simply appalling, as is the technique used. While Chairman of Selectors I tried to get some information regarding baseball technique and the reduction of injuries it entails, and Micky Stewart tells me that my efforts then are just beginning to bear fruit. It might only be at the junior levels, but if we can get good habits into the youngsters, it should not be long before they start to infiltrate the game as a whole.

The biggest breakthrough in fielding skills that I ever saw came from Colin Bland. The first time I had a personal introduction to his skills was in South Africa in 1965 when he ran me out in Port Elizabeth by some seven or eight yards. I pushed the ball for a single and suddenly there was an explosion at the other end as the stumps simply disappeared with me miles short of making my ground. That was his trademark. He developed the one-handed pick-up and throw to hit the stumps, not merely find the 'keeper's gloves as had usually been the case. Since the introduction of the third umpire and the TV replays, we have been able to see how much time is lost by the wicket-keeper having to take the bails off, however close the throw is to them. Without the benefits of TV replays, I just wonder how many times umpires gave batsmen not out when Colin Bland hit the stumps, merely because it all happened too quickly for the naked eye?

One-day cricket has obviously had an effect on fielding, with the advent of the sliding stop among the major innovations. White trousers become greener and browner than they ever used to, and nobody gets his whites dirtier quicker than Jonty Rhodes. He has probably developed the technique to the optimum point where he comes up out of the slide into a throwing position and completes the manoeuvre all in one fluid movement. It is a question of balance, strength, and, all-important, practice.

When we talk about enthusiasm, there is no better example than Derek Randall. It was fun to watch him field for he obviously considered it to be fun. He would spend most of the day trying to engineer a run-out, and when it eventually happened, his uninhibited glee was there for all to see. Derek did not have a particularly

JONTY RHODES: *Nobody gets his whites dirtier.*

strong arm from the outfield, but he was a wonderfully quick mover over the ground and had a nice quick accurate throw.

Some of the quick bowlers have had good arms, but perhaps the best I ever saw was Norman O'Neill. Again, the Australian had learnt his technique in baseball, and that allowed him to become the only man I have seen throw the ball in relatively flat from the straight boundaries at Adelaide. That means a carry of some 100 yards or more. While others needed relays to return it, Norman could get it back in one go. Of the fast bowlers, you had to admire the throwing arm of the West Indian Charlie Griffith – if only when he was in the field. When one had slight doubts about the legality of his bowling action, it put a slight chill into proceedings when you saw him pick the ball up on an eighty-five yard boundary and, with a minimum of effort, send it straight back low and flat.

There is no doubt that Englishmen suffer in comparison with the Australians. They are forever getting injured 'throwing their arm out', whatever that entails. Again, I tried to enlist American knowledge, but medical inertia took over. Baseball pitchers do get plenty of time to warm up, whereas a cricket fielder can stand there for an hour at a time on a cold outfield and then suddenly be expected to be close to peak performance. However, I am quite sure they get the pitchers back into action quickly if they do ever throw their arms out. When we have learned all we can from their medical men, we need to study technique. From a quick glance, baseball players return from the outfield with the hand always vertical and straight over the shoulder. If you try to get any sort of distance going round the shoulder, you are in the wrong slot.

Baseball throwers do seem to take their time. They set themselves to throw but that is time well spent. The quick, off-balance throw might deter the batsmen from taking a second run because the ball is already in the air. However, a study of effectiveness would, I believe, show significant results. That is not necessarily the case with West Indians, who tend to be good at it, but again the poor old Englishman is shown up as being second best. Recently, however, there has been some research which suggests that the old, loopy throw from the outfield is not the most effective. It has been found that skidding the ball in first bounce gets it back much quicker.

There are other facets of fielding in which the Englishman can hold his head up along with the best of them. It is fair to say that our slip fielders stand comparison with most, and that is at a time when a greater proportion of catches are held today than in my time. I am not sure why that should be, because we used to practise a fair amount. It might just be that nowadays, with television close-ups, there is an imperative to catch them, otherwise you look such a mug. They do still get dropped, and I was interested to hear a Pakistani claim that the reason they dropped so many in Australia was that they are not used to the bouncy pitches. At home, not many edges would have carried to the slips.

We have, of course, a reputation for fine wicket-keepers in England, as seen by Jack Russell setting a new standard for catches in a Test in South Africa. However, perhaps the most inventive piece of wicket-keeping I have seen was by the great Godfrey Evans. A lively medium-pace bowler slipped in a ball of full yorker length which appeared to go under the batsman's feet. He had a big swish at it as he fell, getting his feet out of the way, and in the middle of this flurry came a big appeal for a stumping. Godfrey had taken the ball left-handed and had jammed it up against the base of the leg-stump. Not many 'keepers other than Godfrey could have contemplated such a move, let alone got the stumping.

Godfrey was a great motivator, always conducting the efforts of the fielders. Perhaps in that respect he was ahead of his time, for clapping and encouragement is very much part of the modern game. In fact it sometimes worries me that a young lad making his Test début can be out there in the front of the clappers and the motivators. If that sort of thing had happened in my day and I was told by a newcomer to sharpen up my act, I might just have found a few suitable words to say to him in return.

The Captain's Shoulders

The cricket captain has, arguably, the most powerful position in any sport. The mere fact that cricket goes on for such a long period gives it a special quality and makes serious demands both on and off the field. Man-management, technical advice, and the creation of an aura of confidence for your team are all contributory factors in the making of a good captain. Furthermore, the man chosen has to gain the respect of his team, for there will be times when it all goes wrong. If the team still believes that what you have done is for the best, even when things go horribly wrong, the captain has created the right atmosphere.

The weaker captain, or one who is undermined, is in an unenviable position. That is when one or two players start to get ideas about what might have gone wrong, and I can remember instances when senior players were naughty: at the time when the captain needs support, they sit in the corner muttering things like 'What do they expect if they send us a boy to do a man's job?' It was usually the young captain who tended to be a bit vulnerable to such gossip. When things were going well, he was a hero; when the going got a bit tricky, the old pros would get together in the slips and the muttering would begin.

Inspirational captains are few and far between, but Richie Benaud had the ability to get Australia out of a mess on a few occasions by maintaining a genuine confidence which rubbed off on other people. His man-management was excellent, as seen by the fact that he continually managed to get Alan Davidson on the field despite his being one of the greatest hypochondriacs the game has seen.

Looking at the really successful captains, you had the hard men, with Clive Lloyd going pretty near the top of that list. Welfare of the opposition was not among his top priorities. Michael Brearley has a great reputation as a psychologist, without a peer in man-management. Certainly he had style on the field and you could see that he was in control. He got the best out of Ian Botham, but there is also the need to be lucky as a captain as well as good. There have been captains who win a lot more tosses than others, and there have been the unlucky ones. J. M. Brearley definitely has to come into the fortunate category, for you only have to ask how England came to be 500–1 against at Headingley in 1981. You might say that if he was such a good captain, he would not have let his side get into such a position, but the proof of his ability is the getting out of it.

With Brearley, it was not just a one-off either, for in the next match at Edgbaston he did it again. I remember sitting in the commentary box and thinking what the odds might be this time. To get out of jail twice, or three times if you include Old Trafford, does suggest that he had special qualities. Perhaps he was lucky that he did have Ian Botham regularly performing feats of the utmost heroism, but it was the captain who created the atmosphere in which such acts could be successful.

CLIVE LLOYD: *Welfare of the opposition was not among his top priorities.*

He also had the fortune to be coming up against an Australian captain, Kim Hughes, who was not as hard as some others.

Ian Chappell, by contrast, delighted in the hard man and hard captain image. One of his players, Ross Edwards, told me how Chappell regenerated Edwards's fielding ability. He was a fine cover-point, quite capable of judging where he should be positioned, but on this occasion he had been told where to go. Nevertheless, the batsman was hitting it squarer for four. Edwards kept looking at his captain, suggesting that he might move a little to his left. If Chappell noticed, he did not let on. Finally he plucked up the courage to suggest that he might be better deployed slightly squarer. The answer he got was something along the lines of 'Go where you *@+*ing well like, you stupid little *@+*!' Chappell turned on his heels and left Edwards to make the decision. He took it as a vote of confidence in his fielding ability and cricket awareness.

Of the captains under whom I played, Peter May was the great encourager. He treated different people as individuals, and always gave them encouragement. At the time, I was not a particularly disciplined bowler, but I could move the ball around and acquired a reputation for being able to break a partnership. As a stand developed, he would keep me interested, suggesting that the time would soon be ripe for my brand of bowling. Eventually, he would say, 'Come on, Ted, it's time to get that fruit box ball out of the closet.' It might have come in the form of a high full-toss or a wide half-volley, but it would have the effect of beating the batsman and giving Peter his wicket. By treating me with a certain amount of humour, he knew he would get the best out of me.

Looking at England's present-day captain I feel that Michael Atherton is getting there, although he was very green at the outset. He seemed to spend long periods about ten minutes behind the game, but he is now getting up to speed, perhaps under the influence of Raymond Illingworth who was absolutely excellent as a technician on the field. He was usually an over in front of the game and moulded an unlikely assortment of individuals into an Ashes-winning team in 1970–71. Indeed, we are lucky with the Test captains around the world at the moment: good men with the right attitude to the game who will ensure that it is played in the proper spirit for some years to come. That is, providing they adhere to their principles when things go wrong. That is when the weight of the world falls upon the captain's shoulders and he is in the loneliest position imaginable. Perhaps it is no bad idea to be captain before becoming a Chairman of Selectors; one position is good training for the other.

The Art of Selection

There are many who believe that the best selection committees are those which consist of one person. That selector can then follow his own instinct and select his favourite players. Such a situation rarely exists in cricket and teams are picked by a group of selectors who all bring their own ideas to the meeting. People might not realise quite how dynamic a selection meeting can be. At the end of such a meeting, the selectors will usually have agreed on the team with the exception of only a couple of places, yet those selections are the ones which cause the problems.

It is fair to say that most people in the game could write down about eight names at the outset of a selection meeting and get them right. Then there is a tactical element about how the circle will be squared – is it going to be this bowler or that one, or, will the all-rounder play? It always struck me that the players who do eventually take the field should be those in the best possible frame of mind as opposed to being absolutely right for those last three places. The mere fact that they were not automatic selections means that they are going to be fringe players, whoever they are. Having the man with the right approach and in form is much more important.

Amateur selectors should beware. The captain and manager are those who know the players well enough to assess how they are feeling, and how they are likely to perform on the day. It is more important to look at general trends and overall quality rather than just to claim that, when a selection differs from yours, it is a bad selection. However, it is inevitable that, if the chosen side does not win, it is always because the selection is regarded as faulty. A player never has a bit of bad luck nor does he fall victim to a brilliant piece of cricket by the opposition; he is always the wrong player. The reverse is not true. When the selectors go for a player who succeeds, the choice was always obvious in the eyes of the public. How many times have you heard anybody say, 'That was a brave selection but a damned good one because this chap can really play?' The only time I can remember hearing that was in 1975 in the case of David Steele.

The beauty of the job is that every selection is different and every set of circumstances is different. You have to be aware that you are picking a team and not just a collection of individuals. You want continuity to give everybody a fair chance, yet the pressure for change can become irresistible when the team loses. You also want to play your best eleven, if such a notion exists, but you cannot afford to have a whole generation growing old together. Sometimes you strike lucky with a selection, more often you feel desperately let down – despite the fact that the player has tried his best it has not worked out for him. Selection is far from being an exact science.

The Mysteries of the LBW Law

It is not surprising that part-time cricket followers sometimes fail to understand the intricacies of the LBW Law, because in about twenty per cent of cases commentators on radio and television get it wrong when talking about the merits or otherwise of a decision. It is important, however, to look at the historical development of the Law to gain a wider sense of the present legislation.

Until 1744 the batsman was allowed to kick the ball away from the wicket with impunity, except for a painful blow on the shin; but then the umpires were empowered to prevent batsmen 'standing unfair to strike'. By 1774, the batsman was out if 'he puts his leg before the wicket with a design to stop the ball from hitting the wicket'. An amendment was introduced in 1788 which stipulated that the ball had to be pitched in a straight line between wicket and wicket and to be travelling to hit the stumps, but the 1774 clause concerning intention was omitted. An insignificant experiment was staged between 1929 and 1933, whereby a batsman could still be out LBW even if the ball hit the bat on the way to the pad, and it was not until 1937 that a major change took place to the 1788 ruling. After a two-year experiment, it was decided that the Law would include balls pitching outside off-stump providing the point of contact between ball and pad was between wicket and wicket.

This meant that if the ball pitched outside the off stump, the batsman really had to be going back if the ball was to make impact between wicket and wicket and be going to hit the stumps. It still did not prevent the batsman going forward to anything pitching outside the off-stump and simply kicking it away. That practice had become so prevalent by 1970 that an experimental ruling was introduced whereby a batsman could be given out LBW, even if the point of impact was outside off-stump, if he made no attempt to play the ball. It was accepted officially in 1972 and was embodied in the MCC's re-codified version of The Laws in 1980.

This demanded that the umpires had to be pretty sharp at judging the various angles involved. Was the ball seaming, or turning far enough in to hit the stumps? Was it doing so much that it would miss leg-stump? Was it going over the top? All these questions had to be answered, as well as the intent clause which had reappeared for the first time since 1788. In essence, there had been three stages in producing the Law as it stands today.

Because of the original, pre-1973 Law, if a bowler was to be effective he had to ensure that his delivery was travelling wicket to wicket. The moment it came from any angle outside the off-stump, the batsman could play back with impunity. If it was at all short, it had to be pitching outside off if it was to hit the stumps. It was a formal invitation to the batsman to pull because, even if the ball kept low, he could not be out.

So, who were the most successful bowlers? Of the quicker variety, those who went close to the stumps and who managed to shape the ball away from the right-hander. That would ensure they could prevent the ball from running down the leg side despite the fact that it had pitched on the stumps. If a natural in-swing bowler appeared, it would not be long before his coach or schoolmaster suggested that he was not destined for much success unless he changed his action and basic delivery.

Leg-spinners could obviously be reasonably successful, pitching leg-stump and hitting off. I also remember, even in my time, left-arm spinners bowling round-the-wicket being told to run very close to the stumps, and arching their backs. This gave them a line which involved pitching on the wicket and just turning away a little bit, even when there was not much turn to be had, so as not to run down the leg-side. Off-break bowlers also tended to get in very close to the stumps, trying to achieve the same objectives and, by getting their front foot landing across the wicket, they could ensure their arm came over absolutely straight down the line. If there was a bit of turn, the off-spinner would go around the wicket, again close to the stumps, so he could pitch on line and be hitting the stumps.

Suddenly, someone has the bright idea to change the Law so that a ball pitching outside off-stump can now gain a LBW decision. But not every bowler, however, is going to be able to change his approach overnight to take advantage of that change. What happened was that different types of bowler came along. That young lad with the big in-swinging action who had little future in the game is suddenly the most successful bowler in the school. The master-in-charge of cricket no longer tells him to change, but pats him on the back and tells him how well he is doing. He gets plenty of bowling, develops his art, and becomes very good at what he is doing.

Now that the ball can pitch outside off-stump, there is a completely different set of parameters that a bowler can use. The quick bowler does not have to get close to the stumps any more, which is evident when you watch one of the most successful, Allan Donald. This allows bowlers to generate a lot of momentum over the crease. They no longer had to check at the stumps, perhaps pivoting a little to get away again, but could just run straight through. A new generation of what might be termed 'run through' bowlers emerged, like Malcolm Marshall, with a lot of pace over the ground and then a very quick arm. He had many other splendid attributes, but certainly on English pitches he could get batsmen playing a good foot to eighteen inches outside off-stump. They had to in case the ball came back sharply enough to hit the stumps.

Just playing back was no longer really an option, nor was just playing along the line of the stumps. It might also be that the helmet is a long-term consequence of the LBW Law. Batsmen felt that the only way to be sure is to get forward with the pad in line with the ball. The moment they started playing forward to high-class fast bowling, they needed the extra protection of the helmet. Perhaps the same process has led to the alarming increase in the incidence of broken fingers and the developments which have taken place in glove design.

In 1972, when the regulation appeared, the main

grouse came from Australia on the basis that the googly bowler was being penalised. The batsman would go back to cut what he thought was a leg-spinner, it transpired it was a googly and, because he was playing a stroke and had got just outside the line of off-stump, he was not out. Of course, the people it helped more than anyone else were the fast bowlers. They were the ones who benefited from batsmen playing the ball at an unwarranted distance outside the off-stump.

Of the bowlers who happened to come into their own through a means of natural selection after the rule change, Derek Underwood must be high on the list. Although 'Deadly' made his début in 1963 and took 101 wickets in his first season of county cricket, he would have been growing up in the late 1950s. A young lad bowling medium-pace cutters, left-arm, from fairly wide of the wicket, would have got a fair degree of success. He was always very accurate, which is important for schoolboys, so nobody stopped him from doing what he did successfully and so he developed his skills. He had reached the top when suddenly a new regulation comes into existence which falls right into his lap. He bowled a really good arm-ball which came ripping in from way out wide and would also turn away from a right-handed batsman. It was guaranteed to get batsmen playing at balls they should be leaving alone.

The question of how to combat the high-class quick bowler who bowls it wide on the basis that the odd one will come back is an interesting one. Batsmen took the view that they had to get forward, but I have seen enough

DEREK UNDERWOOD: He bowled a really good arm-ball which came ripping in from way out wide and would also turn away from a right-handed batsman.

now to know that it is six of one and half a dozen of the other. In fact, I am sure that they would be better off not just plunging forward. Doing that means they play at balls they should not play, they edge them when they would not if they played more in line with their stumps, and they get hit more, thereby giving the bowler the ascendancy. I think the tried and trusted technique of playing back and across, get into line and stay on the back foot until you see where the ball is, is still by and large the most successful. It is certainly the way the best players of fast bowling still do it. If the bowler is good enough to 'do' you with the one pitching outside off and coming back, well, so be it. He is probably good enough to do you anyway.

There have been other knock-on effects from the change in the LBW Law in 1970. There was, for a long period, the virtual disappearance of leg-slips and backward short-legs to the fast bowlers. In fact, one or two of these endangered species have been spotted again, but if the line of attack is a foot outside off-stump there is not much call for them. On the other hand, I do wonder, if they placed men over there, whether the bowlers would not pitch the ball up at the stumps a little more. That might get the ball to swing more, the bat might be off-line and you might just get a few more edges into that area.

The other thing that has happened has been the development of the technique against slow bowling whereby the pad is thrust at the ball with the bat brought in behind the pad. In truth, there is little actual intent to play the ball with the bat. However, it is used as a device to deter the umpire from giving a decision in favour of the bowler on the basis that the batsman was attempting to play a stroke but, unfortunately, the pad got in the way of the bat striking the ball. A lot of us have thought that the umpires have been a little timid, especially when such a ploy is repeated over after over. However, the Law as written insists that the ball would have been going to hit the stumps if it had not been intercepted. The interpretation has been established whereby the umpires judge that, if the ball had not struck the pad, it would still not have hit the wicket because the bat was in line to prevent it from doing so.

It might well be that this could be another useful change to the Law. The wording would need to be looked at closely, but something which got rid of the boring defence mechanism would be a good contribution. It would need only to change the umpires' attitude to increase more positive batting against the spinners. That, in turn, would encourage the slow bowlers and that is something which we on the relevant committees have been desperately trying to do. We appreciate the importance of maintaining the variety of the game so that it does not become the exclusive domain of fast bowlers.

The MCC Cricket Committee is responsible for the framing of The Laws to interpret what players actually want. The Laws, of course, must be for all cricket, not just for the higher echelons of the game, which makes the task quite difficult. If we propose something that is not liked by a section of the game, they merely draft in a special playing condition to circumvent our regulation. We have, however, put together a statement to go before the first-ever meeting of the Test captains. We state that we cherish the variety in the game and all developments which tend towards only one aspect are to be deplored. We ask captains therefore, particularly in their role as selectors, to be mindful of the greater good; but I am not convinced they will pay too much heed to our high ideals when faced with the realities of winning a Test match.

What is important is that we at least show our intentions. Those of us charged with being guardians of the game take our responsibilities seriously. If our urgings are not acknowledged, we might then be forced to take legislative measures to impose them. That is not as easy as it might seem. It is obvious, for instance, that any tampering with the LBW Law has far-reaching implications, all of which would have to be considered but not all of which could possibly be anticipated. Nevertheless, the time might come when an amendment will be in order to encourage the game to develop along the right lines.

Playing in the Old-Fashioned Way

Michael Atherton is an orthodox batsman who continually acts as an example which proves that the traditional attributes of good batting still work. He is an opening batsman of the highest quality and in 1995 was probably the only England player who would be able to secure a place in a World XI. Furthermore, he is unique in one other sense.

Virtually all his contemporaries in the England team had the benefit of a word or two from the then Chairman of Selectors. I talked to the likes of Graham Thorpe, Graeme Hick, Mark Ramprakash and Alec Stewart about their batting on more than one occasion. Thorpe certainly, I remember, on an England 'A' tour had a tendency to plunge forward to the slow bowlers. I persuaded him to play back and murder them. Usually, however, I would only talk to batsmen when they were on the verge of getting dropped. Alec Stewart was one of those. I remember that, on one of the few occasions I got to talk to Graeme Hick, he was very cautious and unreceptive so I did not pursue the matter.

I tried to get Mark Ramprakash to stay more sideways in the stroke when I took him into a net. I threw balls at him and got him to move both forward and back with some success in that he was beginning to hit the ball so much more sweetly. At the end of it I asked him how it felt. His answer was 'different'. His later problems were caused by reverting to his old style, getting too square in the stroke, with his left shoulder going one way and the bat the other.

I did talk to Michael Atherton about his batting, but never suggested any changes. I remember particularly on his first trip to Australia when I was Chairman of Selectors, I went to the nets in Sydney and was horrified by what I saw. One England batsman after another was completely inept from a technical point of view. I almost felt ashamed to have selected them. We recruited some Australian left-arm bowlers to come into the nets to try and give the batsmen practice before facing Bruce Reid. They responded by getting bowled and nicking it with bats coming down far from straight. The only one who looked like a player was Michael. He came out of the net and, as he walked past, opened the conversation by asking what I thought. I told him to keep doing what he was doing because he looked so sound. He played straight, left the ones that could be left, and proceeded to get a hundred in that match. I was pleased I had not tried any magic on him.

The only other time I had a chat to him about his game, I like to think that I might have given him a little food for thought, at least. It was at a time when Alec Stewart was on the verge of getting dropped from the team. He had not only had a run of low scores, but did not seem to be going about things the right way either. To complicate the situation, Micky Stewart, his father, was the team manager. When I suggested to Alec that he might like me to throw some balls at him in the net and talk about his batting, Micky made to come as well.

172

I said that we did not want father interfering and, seeing Michael Atherton, suggested that he might like to come along to throw the balls for me.

I was trying to get Alec into slightly different positions, notably not getting quite so much behind the ball when he tended to get squared up. If he kept to the side of the ball, he could let it come up to him; if he was right behind it, he had no option but to play it in front of him. Having made the point to Alec, Michael was again the inquiring one as we walked back from the nets. He wanted to know more about the idea of letting the ball come up to the batsman and playing it more underneath the head. I explained that, quite simply, all the good batsmen I had ever seen had played that way.

R. E. S. Wyatt was the great one for saying that the place to watch batsmen was from the side. You could tell their quality, or lack of it, by looking to see the position of the point of impact with the bat. The more they let it come up, the better players they would be. When following Bob Wyatt's dictum, some batsmen play the ball surprisingly far forward. It is interesting to note that all those shots which Michael plays best appear to be played very late. When he plays the ball down through the third-man area, he would be a real candidate to give a catch to the slips if he pushed at the ball at all. However, he does not push, he lets the ball come and, with good control and soft hands, he runs the ball away safely. Playing back, he is a fine example of the old adage 'Don't get behind it; get beside it.' He does get a bit square-on when playing forward, but then nobody is perfect.

Technically Mike holds his positions very well on the back strokes. His footwork is not always absolutely copybook and it could be said to be limited. However, he knows what he is doing, moving on to his front foot first, but not going so far across as to allow that foot to get in the way. The key to his batting is a very straight pick-up. The bat does not come down from gully. He might not completely open the blade, not being a natural hooker or puller even though he does sometimes get such a shot away. He turns the ball well off his hip, but his great strength is square on the off side, either with the cover-drive, when he really makes a study of the shot, or his square-drive with a straight bat off the back foot. It might seem that he is a little limited in his stroke repertoire, but he is an accumulator of the soundest type. This soundness gives him confidence and once he has lasted for an hour, he sees little reason why he should not last for another and another.

At the start of his Test career, not many people would have backed Michael Atherton to do as well as he has. Clearly his absolute guts and concentration have been a major factor in his success. More than once I have felt that the fast bowlers might have got through to him, yet he still comes back for more in a most wonderful way. My lasting impression of him is the moment after a bouncer has whistled past his nose. He looks four-square up the wicket with a flinty look in his eye, impressing his own personality on the bowler and driving himself on to the next challenge. It is a marvellous sight, and he should be hugely commended for what he has achieved.

In the first England 'A' team which went to Zimbabwe, he was clearly the outstanding player. He went on from there to fulfil what everyone who saw him on that tour suggested he would. He had the nickname 'FEC' when he was at Cambridge, for he was easily identifiable as the Future England Captain. When he was appointed, during my term as Chairman of Selectors, it was a very close thing between Michael and Alec Stewart. I am sure Alec would have proved perfectly capable and was the senior man, whereas Michael was not an established captain at county level. In the long term, I am sure we made the right decision.

It is always interesting to compare one generation of players with another, and I ask myself the question whether Atherton would have got into the England sides in which I played. Looking back to a time when there were some outstanding batsmen in the England team, I believe he would have found a place, as we were a little short of openers of the highest quality until Geoff Boycott came along. There was a long list of batsmen who opened the innings for England in Tests at the time, with some unlikely names among them. Men like Raymond Illingworth, Fred Titmus, Jimmy Binks, and John Murray do not readily come to mind as Test openers, but they had a go at the job along with a host of established openers. There were few solid partnerships because I can remember that, as number three, I was frequently facing the new ball. Michael Atherton would have fitted very well into those sides.

The important point is that he would not have looked

out of place in terms of technique alongside some of the leading names of English cricket. So many modern

MICHAEL ATHERTON: Almost alone amongst modern English batsmen, he has shown that an orthodox way of playing produces consistent success.

batsmen fail to establish themselves at the highest level because they have flaws in technique or temperament, or both. Those who do survive have tended to do so by compensating for self-imposed problems in technique. Michael Atherton, almost alone amongst modern English batsmen, has shown that an orthodox way of playing produces consistent success. There are eternal truths in cricket, and it is satisfying for those of us brought up to play that way to see the application of the simple, basic elements of the game bringing results.

Perhaps, with Michael Atherton's success in our minds, there will be a widespread acceptance that a return to orthodoxy is the best way – perhaps the only way – for English cricket to progress.

Index

Page numbers in *italic* refer to illustrations

O'Neill, Norman
  125, 151

Packer, Kerry 102, 132
Palmer, Ken 126
Parkhouse, Gilbert 20
Parks, Jim 108
Patterson 90
Pollock, Graeme 114
Pollock, Peter 57–8
Prabhakar, Manoj 96
Prasanna, Erapally 13
Pringle, Derek 123
Procter, Mike 146

Qadir, Abdul 114

Ramadhin, Sonny 13–14
Ramprakash, Mark 64,
  123, 149, 171
Randall, Derek 150–1
Reid, Bruce 172
Reid, John 9
Rhodes, Jonty 150, *151*
Richards, Viv 62–4, *63*
Roberts 89
Robins, R.W.V. 132
Robinson, Ian 126
Rorke 87
Russell, Jack 96,
  121, 153

Sheppard, Rev. David 21
Simpson, Bobby 15, 60,
  84, 111–12
Slade, Doug 40
Smith, Robin 16, *16*,
  34, 134–5
Snow, John 146
Sobers, Sir Garfield 52,
  68–74, *71*, 96, 128
Sohail, Aamir 126
Statham, Brian 65,
  144–5, *145*
Steele, Bob 121
Steele, David 161
Stewart, Alec 28, 171,
  172–3, 175
Stewart, Micky 46, 61,
  149, 172
Surridge, Stuart 8

Taylor, Mark 46–7
Thomson, Alan 'Froggy'
  76
Thomson, Jeff 52,
  77, *78*, 80
Thorpe, Graham 83–4,
  137, 171
Titmus, Fred 12, 40, 175
Trueman, Fred 23–7, *24*,
  78, 125, 146
Tufnell, Philip
  41–2